ECHOES OF AFRICA

ECHOES OF
AFRICA

Dennis and Ena Fowler

Matador
9 Priory Business Park,
Wistow Road, Kibworth Beauchamp,
Leicestershire. LE8 0RX
Tel: 0116 279 2299
Email: books@troubador.co.uk
Web: www.troubador.co.uk/matador
Twitter: @matadorbooks

ISBN 978 1784624 323

British Library Cataloguing in Publication Data.
A catalogue record for this book is available from the British Library.

Typeset in 11pt Aldine401 BT Roman by Troubador Publishing Ltd, Leicester, UK

Matador is an imprint of Troubador Publishing Ltd

To Ena, who walked, waded, paddled and drove all the way with me,
and unlike me, faced danger and death on several occasions
with trust in the Lord.

CONTENTS

FOREWORD

*T*his little book is based primarily on weekly letters which I wrote to my mother from Northern Rhodesia over a period of nearly eight years. When Ena and I left Zambia in 1966, I often regretted not having kept a diary, as the memories of our life as missionaries became faded and confused. When my mother died in 1979, I was surprised to receive the letters, which she had faithfully kept over the years.

Last year I used the letters to write about our experiences, as the record of a long-lost way of life. It soon became clear that I could not do this alone. I needed Ena, as always, to polish out the crudities of style, to correct the errors of fact and mistaken recollection, to fill out the many gaps where her own experiences supplemented mine, and not least to add an appendix on the Ila language, where her work had broken new ground. Her work has been indicated where ever it stands in the memoir.

PROLOGUE

O n the wall of the Sunday school at Abbey Methodist Church in
Barrow-in-Furness was a large coloured print of Jesus, surrounded
by children of many races. It was noticeable that the little African
boy seemed apart from the rest, sitting on the ground, with face averted.

On the sideboard in our house in Barrow was a handsome wooden
collecting box labelled "Junior Missionary Association". As a JMA member,
I used to pester all my relations for money to pay for missionary work. I
still have a biography of Sam Pollard, the pioneer missionary, bearing a
handsome gold label inside its gaudy orange cover:

> *Abbey Road Methodist Sunday School*
> *This is to certify that Dennis Fowler has*
> *collected during the year 1941 the*
> *sum of £ - : 13s : 2d for missionary work*
> *overseas and at Home*

I suppose, with hindsight, that what follows was inevitable.

TRAVELLING TO AFRICA

*I*n January 1958, Ena and I sailed away to Africa. We did not take the pith helmets and clerical evening dress recommended on the kit list provided by the Methodist Missionary Society. We did take an 80-year-old sewing machine, a heavy hunting rifle, a revolver, 24 tea-chests of books, a steel trunk full of clothes, 12 dozen vacuum snap closures for bottling jam, 12 dozen giant bales of cotton wool, and a six-week-old daughter.

We travelled in a manner strange to the jet age of these days. After a fortnight at sea, we landed at Cape Town and boarded the train to the interior, which trundled north at 25 mph for a further four days, with a break at Bulawayo station. We bathed little Rebecca daily in the tiny wash basin and shed a fresh layer of garments each day.

When we finally reached Kafue Training Institute we found that the Methodist Missionary Society had forgotten to notify anybody of our coming. This did not really surprise us, because we already realised that the training course for missionaries in Northern Rhodesia had advised us to study the wrong language.

Fortunately the *Cape Town Argus* always published the passenger lists of every Union Castle arrival, so that Winston Jubb, the Principal of the school, learned of our existence soon after we docked at Cape Town:

The Reverend Dennis Fowler, Mrs. Ena Fowler, Miss Rebecca Fowler, travelling to Kafue Training Institute, N. Rhodesia.

Winston, the Principal of Kafue Training Institute, hastily converted an old grass-roofed mud-walled hut into temporary quarters for us. When the baby cried on the first night, Ena was almost too frightened to cross the floor and

Our hut at Kafue

feed her, for fear of things dropping on to us out of the thatch. Not a promising start!

We spent 18 months at Kafue, where I trained primary teachers. Then Synod launched us into the wilderness.

KASENGA

*K*asenga Mission adjoined the ruins of Ibamba Ranch, which Dale, the District Commissioner at Namwala, had built in 1910. Andrew Dale was called "Mopani", the hardest of trees, because of the ruthless way in which he had subdued the Matabele rebellion in the 1890s, and gradually rooted out the chronic inter-tribal warfare. He was a famous hunter and a respected administrator. Paradoxically, he was also a fine scholar and writer, collaborating with Edwin Smith to produce the classic "Ila-speaking Peoples of Northern Rhodesia". He fell in love with an Ila woman and married her according to the solemn rites and ceremonies of Ila custom. He bought a plot of land in 1910 in order to establish a home for his new bride, and called it Ibamba.

When war came in 1914, he enlisted and was badly wounded in the trenches in Europe. He had to leave the Army, returning to his work as a District Commissioner. In 1919 he died of Spanish flu, leaving his wife pregnant, and Ibamba Ranch abandoned. The colonial government did not recognise Dale's Ila marriage, and his wife returned to her village to raise her little son as a Mwila boy.

In the 'twenties Wynant Hubbard, an American scientist and animal researcher, acquired Ibamba Ranch in order to study animal behaviour. He selected it after extensive travel as the area which had more lions and Buffalo than anywhere else in Africa. His object was to explore the possibility of domesticating wild and savage beasts. Hubbard raised several lion cubs from birth in his home, exactly like human children. The famous scene in the film "Tarzan and his mate" that showed Johnny Weissmuller wrestling with a lion was filmed on site at Ibamba in 1934 using one of the tame lions. The Hubbards were on very friendly terms with John and Florence Price, the missionaries next door at Kasenga. The Hubbards' work was going ahead successfully, when Ibamba was devastated by an invasion of locusts, and they were forced to abandon the place in 1939, and return to the USA. Ibamba remained a place of ruins and desolation for many years. (Meanwhile, John Price had traced Mapani Dale's little boy, and educated him at the Mission school, thus laying the foundation for a distinguished career as Provincial Commissioner. We met Andrew Dale Junior in Oxford in 2005, where he had come for an eye operation. He was an imposing figure, tall and ramrod straight, with a magnificent white moustache).

On arrival at Kasenga, we were warmly welcomed by a sponge cake which the two young lady teachers had baked. We were rather taken aback, however, to see in the veranda of the house a large amount of luggage belonging to our immediate predecessors, who had taken one look and hastened away without unpacking, leaving us to send it all back to the railway. We were equally surprised to find a splendid porcelain WC, sitting naked and unashamed in the middle of the back garden, 120 miles from the nearest sewer. A rusty 1928 Ford model A, almost hidden by weeds, hinted at frustration and despair. At last we were in Ila country!

THE ILA PEOPLE

We knew a bit about the people to whom we had been sent. They were called *Bashukulumpo* by David Livingstone, who had made a long detour in order to avoid entering their territory. In *King Solomon's Mines,* Rider Haggard chose their country as the romantic and remote setting for his great adventure story: "Lad, did you ever hear of the Suliman Mountains up in the north-west of the Masukulumbwe country? That is where Solomon really had his mines". They preferred to call themselves "Baila" ("The People"). They had formerly numbered about 25,000, before being ravaged by an outbreak of VD. The government set up a vaccination campaign, and their numbers had risen to around 20,000 by the 1960s. They still did not venture to name new born children until they had lived through their first year. They lived a pastoral life on the Kafue Flats. The men were tall and imposing in appearance, and used to dress their hair in cones almost 4ft high, to show above the tall grass when fighting Lozi raiders. They knocked out the middle front teeth, "in order to avoid being mistaken for zebras". They never travelled even the shortest distance without one or two 8ft spears over their shoulders. They were a warlike and turbulent people. Until the arrival of the Methodist missionaries in the 1890s, no European had been able to settle in their country, and several who attempted to do so had been killed.

This much we knew before our arrival. Later I found in the office a large cupboard, stuffed with a mass of papers and cards. These proved to be a collection of notes on Ila vocabulary, dating back to Edwin Smith's arrival in 1902. He had apparently noted each new word and phrase, and asked one of his local workers to use it in a sentence, which he jotted down on any available paper. His successors had followed this practice. Soon they were writing not only single words or phrases, but songs, stories, proverbs, and interviews with elders. What had started as random jottings on vocabulary expanded over 60 years into an enormous collection of remarks and observations on a wide variety of topics, written or typed on postcards, diary pages, envelopes, cut-up Italian Bible Society forms, and British South Africa Company notepaper. There were over 12,000 items. When we eventually left Kasenga, we took the papers home to England in two battered suitcases. If only we had known all this at the start of our work!

We unpacked and began to get acquainted with our parishioners, who soon turned up to have a look at us. The first was a man with toothache, who asked me to extract the painful tooth. "I'm sorry, but you need special forceps for that", I replied confidently. "Muluti Price always kept them in that cupboard", he told me helpfully. My bluff was called, and I had to admit that I was totally unable to draw teeth, whatever the instruments. He stalked away in disgust leaving me crestfallen. I had fallen at the first hurdle.

Other early visitors were less demanding. A man brought Ena some six feet of white cloth and asked her to make it into a shroud. Another presented her with a seven-foot spear, and requested that she put it away for him, because he might be tempted to stick it into his nagging wife.

We found Kasenga to be a place of strange beauty. The sky was a great

A place of strange beauty

The tall grass

bowl with a distant circular horizon, broken only by anthills and clumps of palm trees dotted about over the vast plain of grass. Later, when the rain started, we could see mighty thunderclouds approaching from 30 miles away. Herds of buck, zebra and elephant still roamed nearby, so that we were able to manure our garden with elephant dung. Near our house was a lagoon covered with water lilies, on which flamingos lived. When they flew up, the sky was misted by a pink cloud.

Our land was part of the Kafue Game Park, and surrounded by a wire fence. Every time we drove back to the line-of-rail, a guard inspected every inch of the Land Rover with a torch and sprayed us with DDT, to make sure that we were not carrying any of the deadly tsetse flies out of the infected area.

In addition to the fence, a wide fireguard had to be maintained free of grass right round the mission land. The grass grew up to nine feet tall, and had to be cleared every year to keep off the great fires which swept across the plains annually.

Things had changed little at Kasenga since the arrival of the pioneers in 1899. True, we had the Land Rover, but there were still no roads, and when the mighty Kafue River flooded each year the mission gradually became an island in a lake several miles wide. We had to get about by canoe and ox-cart, like our predecessors. There was no electricity, gas, or piped sanitation, and the post and groceries came weekly from Choma, via Jones' Transport bus and our own boat.

Alimon brings the day's water

Filling our water drums

We were awakened daily by Alimon, our herdsman, as he cracked his 30-foot whip to steer the oxen pulling our water-cart from the river, a mile away. The daily ration was fifty gallons, which he poured into two oil drums behind the house. One drum for our bathwater was cradled over a brick fireplace, the water being piped after use into the little vegetable plot. The other drum was for drinking water, which had to be boiled before use. A third drum was for our petrol, and a fourth for paraffin.

Lighting was by paraffin oil. The lanterns, Tilley pressure lamps and Allison burners, were stored in the lamp room away from the house, and needed daily maintenance: the lantern glasses had to be cleaned of soot, the wicks trimmed, and the oil replaced. One day my hands got covered in oil and burst into flame. I dashed out and plunged them into the sand of the path, and Ena bandaged them with bicarbonate of soda.

In the corridor at the rear of the house was a row of storage bins for sugar, flour, potatoes and other bulk supplies. Milk was powdered and came in big tins called "Klim". Over the years we became so accustomed to it that when we reached civilisation fresh milk seemed greatly inferior.

Our lavatory was ten yards from the back door: a little hut over a very deep hole, over which was a wooden seat. This was surprisingly effective from the sanitary aspect, but it had its drawbacks. One morning I lifted the lid, to be attacked by a swarm of wild bees, busy building their new home.

Another time Ena emerged from the door to see a snake on the path just in front of her. At night or in the rainy season or during bouts of malaria it was always an unpleasant experience to go out to the loo.

The windows were protected by mosquito screens, which we were careful to keep in good repair. Every evening, Ena would spray all our rooms liberally with DDT: I can still remember the acrid smell.

We put a net over the cot where Rebecca slept, as an extra protection against mosquitoes. We all took a regular dose of anti-malaria pills. One night we found a black bat creeping across her pillow. Next day we went to Choma and bought a smoke bomb for the chimney, which produced a whole crowd of bats. Badminton rackets were kept handy for any further intruders. In the corner of every room stood a sjambok, a long stiff whip of rhinoceros hide, for killing snakes.

All new houses were built with a zinc ant-course between the ground and the bricks, as the tiniest crack would let in the ants. One evening, a rumbling crash rolled out across the mission. We rushed out, to find Mary Lawrence, a young teacher, standing covered in dust and debris at her front door. It transpired that the ants had found a crack and chewed away the wood frames of the plaster-board walls inside her house, and while she was having a bath the walls had collapsed on to her.

Some insects were harmless or even useful, so we tolerated them. In one top corner of our main room, mason wasps had built their impressive clay home, from which they sailed out to catch flying insects. "Flatties"

Choma, with our Ford

(Selenopidae) lived on the walls. They were rather handsome brown spiders, with their striped legs spread out symmetrically. They remained totally still, like little ornamental plates, until insects crawled near. Our children were fascinated when their papery egg-sacks hatched, and scores of minute but perfect infants emerged. The boys would gently blow on them, and chuckle to see them scuttle madly in all directions. We were always wary of scorpions when putting on shoes, but one day at the start of the rains, I pulled on a welly to find a family of little mice nesting cosily.

Flying ants rose from the ground like jets of smoke at the start of the rains. As they lost their wings and fell to earth, they crawled round in a circle, and the African children fell upon them with delight. They would fill shallow tins with the creatures, and roast them over candles. Apparently they were a tasty source of protein.

Other insects were annoying. Flies bred in millions when the cattle returned from the summer pastures. We had to cover jugs and cups with little muslin doylies, bordered by beads. Only quick gulps were possible before hastily replacing covers on the cups. At night, moths by the dozen would immolate themselves against the hot lamp on the table, to lie charred until swept up next morning.

It was, of course, the mosquitoes that we most feared. They bred by the million on our island, and whenever we ventured out after dusk we took care to wear trousers, which were soon covered with a black rippling mass. Even though we took our pills daily, we could not escape malaria altogether. Ena and I would sometimes be playing delirious chess by lamplight, and the noise of insects would grate on our sharpened nerves like drilling. Our little son Stephen was made deaf by his weekly dose of nivaquin, and we had to change his dose to a daily pill of the bitter paludrin tablets.

Meanwhile, the malaria parasites had taken root inside me, and would persist for many years. A year or two later, I had to go from Choma to Lusaka by motor-bike. On the return journey, I had ridden only a few miles when I felt an attack coming on. I turned back, and just managed to reach the house of my hosts again before collapsing at the door. Fortunately my friend was a nurse. She told me when I came to my senses two days later that my temperature had risen to 106 degrees, and she had had to sponge me constantly hour after hour to bring it down. I cannot remember how I got home on that occasion. I still suffered from bouts 20 years later when we were working in Nazareth.

PRAISE NAMES

*T*he Ila loved nicknames, called "Praise Names". They bestowed them freely on individuals or groups. The Nsante people were called *"Bana-Mwaabane"* (The Dividers), because two villages each claimed the honour of burying a celebrity, so in the end they cut the corpse in two and buried half in each place.

Individuals were picked out with wicked accuracy. *"Musimunakabi"* (She who talks for hours and says nothing) is a universal type. *"Usuba umukome"* (Pisser-on-the-fence) was a timorous man who dared not venture outside the stockade at night.

Missionaries were obvious targets. John Price was *"Cumansingo"* (He wags his head like a stork when he walks) and Dr Gerrard was *"Kabvwelamvuvo"* (Has no favourites). I was merely *"Kapaipi"* (Little man always smoking a pipe), but Ena was *"Sitakatala beenzu"* (She who never tires of receiving visitors). She certainly earned it. From breakfast until dusk, our house was besieged by people seeking Ena. Her praise name could never be used to her face, nor could her Christian name. She was addressed directly as "NuBoome" (Mother), and referred to in the third person as "Batumbu" (Nursing Mother) or "Baina Rebecca" (Rebecca's Mum).

One day a very, very, old lady came to us for refuge. She claimed that she had been beaten by the people of her village, and thrown out as useless. Ena took her in, and made up a bed in my office. From then on, she never let Ena out of her sight, smoking roll ups, and eating hearty meals. After a fortnight of this, even Ena had to take steps for her return. We called in the DC, who took her home and read the riot act to the villagers.

"DOKOTELA" (DOCTOR) ENA

*E*na recalls "We had no medical qualifications at all, but I nevertheless accidentally gained a reputation as a doctor. Our little daughter one day sat on a car battery which Dennis had carelessly placed on the ground while working on the Land-Rover. The Nuns at Namwala clinic, most generous friends, gave him a tin of penicillin gauze, a sheet of which healed Rebecca in no time.

"Shortly afterwards, a woman with a bad leg came to me hopefully. I was appalled to see it covered with big tropical ulcers. I thought I would try penicillin gauze and bandaged the leg from ankle to knee, telling the woman by signs to leave the bandage on and return after six days. The woman duly returned, and I unwrapped the rather soiled bandage. Lo and behold! The ulcers had disappeared! My fame as a doctor spread like wildfire, and the flow of patients began".

Patients walked, they were carried, they were pushed on bicycles. One was tied on to a Y-shaped log and dragged along the ground.

Ena's diagnostic methods were basic but effective. Head? Aspirin; Chest? sulphur pills; Stomach? kaolin. In the rainy season it was even simpler: they all had malaria. In a month our personal malaria pills were finished. We begged another 500 from the nuns at Namwala, and by the end of the rains they also were finished.

Frank Davey, the Medical Officer of the Methodist missionary society, quoted in his book this paragraph from a newsletter Ena wrote:

"We could not sit there with our own personal box of 500 pills while babies were brought to us, children carried on bicycles, and messages sent from those who had collapsed on the way. We started to give out our malaria

Sick boy dragged on a forked branch

pills. In a month they were gone. We begged another 500 from the Roman Catholic nun running a small hospital 20 miles away. In another month these were gone. Fortunately the malaria season came to an end, but now we had ulcers, conjunctivitis, coughs, diarrhoea, burns, and mostly it was children who came, with their parents or alone. We often have the same group of five or six children aged from two to seven who have come all by themselves, with bad ears, bad eyes, ulcers and coughs; they all reel off their ailments, or else a child of five will speak up for one of the younger ones too small to talk".

One day a man came for treatment carrying a bucket which contained his severed left hand. Another man came with a bullet in his stomach. On both these occasions we were away, so they walked on another 20 miles to the nuns at Namwala.

In later years, when the Mission was relocated at New Kasenga, Ena could not cope with the rising numbers – as many as seventy a day. My office was turned into a dispensary, and we employed a trained local girl as part-time nurse. She was paid £11/month, well above the Government rate. We raised funds to pay her and buy medicines by holding a monthly rummage sale of clothes sent by churches and friends in England. This eventually led to the establishment of an official clinic.

Our sales were exciting events. For a month, the postbag brought by

The group of sick children

Jones' Transport was far too small to contain the extra parcels of clothes. We fixed a day for the first sale, and put big notices in the local dealers' stores, announcing the sale for the following Friday at 2:30pm. I piled the clothes inside the church.

Before 6 am the people started arriving, and rows of faces pressed against our dining-room window as we ate breakfast. By 2 pm there were more than 200 people gathered at the church. Little groups kept sneaking away to our house, to try to get a preview or to claim special treatment by reason of their deep friendship to us. Before the auction proper, we admitted about fifteen people to whom we had promised clothes, but between them they took a whole hour to make their selection. Meanwhile I was in front of the church door, trying to keep the crowd at bay. In the end they got so noisy that I decided to conduct the auction from the top of the Mission van instead of inside the church. The crowd which soon assembled round the VW was joined by the passengers and crew of the Jones' Transport bus, who evidently had good noses for a bargain.

The actual selling was conducted somehow in the face of a continuous roar of conversation, comment, abuse, argument and complaint from the

A sale

crowd. In many cases, the bidding did not go as high as it might, because if anyone bid what was considered a fair price for a garment, any attempt to outbid was shouted down with howls of execration. In the end, after three hours, the last garment was sold – even the enormous antique whalebone lace-up corset. The takings were tallied at £16, nearly all of it in small silver. Those who had failed to buy anything had their names recorded; we promised that the date of the next sale would be revealed only to them, in order to limit numbers. We also decided to hold future sales in the early morning and not in the afternoon. We had learned our lesson.

FRIENDS AND NEIGHBOURS

Masonde

Soon after our arrival at Old Kasenga, we were paid a courtesy call by Masonde, the headman of the nearest Ila village, less than half a mile off. He was a tall, lean man almost 80 years old, but straight as a ramrod, with huge ivory bangle on his wrists. He spoke no English, and Ena spoke but little Ila, but they took to each other immediately, and struck up a friendship that lasted for years. He would come almost every morning for a chat on our veranda. He would take out his tobacco-pouch, and Ena would pass him a page of the airmail Times for roll-ups, and there he would sit smoking peacefully. Gradually we learned his story.

Masonde remembered fighting against Lozi cattle-raiders in his days as a young warrior. He recalled the coming of Shmitty (Edwin Smith) and the first missionaries. However, he had surprisingly progressive ideas. The Ila prized their cattle above all things. Their lives revolved around cattle – a typical headstone epitaph would read "He had fifty cattle". Great was the surprise, therefore, when this most senior headman sold his cattle and bought a bright red tractor with the proceeds. Alas, that tractor (chitalakatala)! It stood proudly on a little mound near his house like a monument, and like a monument it never moved, because the brightly-coloured electrical wires of the open engine were too great a temptation to young dandies from miles around, who constantly stole them to weave bracelets.

Masonde gradually lost all his teeth, and went off to Lusaka to get himself fitted with false ones. Everybody was agog to see an Ila warrior with

Masonde

"zebra teeth", but Masonde outwitted us all, and returned with an Ila set, having the front teeth missing, as was proper.

In 1963 after returning from leave in England, we moved to our new mission station, fine modern buildings on the main road to Choma. One day we were touched and delighted to be visited again by Masonde, who had cycled over sandy tracks for 25 miles to see us.

Tony Jones

If Maala was the centre of Ila country, Tony's store was the centre of Maala. It was the staging point to the Mission, the mill for grinding mealies, the general store for a wide range of goods, the information and gossip centre for the whole area, a rest-house and lodging for travellers, and the residence of Tony and his wives. Tony had come to Zambia in the 'twenties, and for some years he and a partner had shot elephants for their tusks. One day, an enraged bull elephant charged them, and his partner's shot failed to stop it. Tony dropped the great beast within a few feet of his partner, saving his life. Instead of thanking him, however, the other man complained bitterly that Tony's bullet had splintered the tusk. "I was so mad", said Tony, "that I gave up hunting on the spot, and decided to open a store instead". When we knew him, Tony was a genial and portly figure, with a store of aphorisms which he loved to quote. "Give us the job, and we'll finish the tools" was one. "Africa goes at the pace of the ox" was another, and "One man, one vote, once".

When Stephen was six weeks old, we had to take him for his third prophylactic injection to Choma Hospital. The journey involved setting off with him and his sister Rebecca, 16 months old, at 6am. The rains were just over, and nursing the Land Rover through the mile of mud and deep pools from our island to Maala was a nightmare. The next 85 miles of sand and mud to the hospital at Choma were slow and laborious. On the return journey in the evening, when we reached Tony's place in Maala, Ena said "I can't face the crossing to the Mission tonight". Tony received us with warm hospitality, with a wash and a hot meal. Meanwhile a junior wife was discreetly moved out of her room behind the store, and we were comfortably installed for the night.

Sometime later, I injured my leg in a spill from my motor-bike. Somehow I managed to ride a few miles to Tony's store. He came out to greet me, and I tried to get my hanky out of my trouser pocket, only to find that my thigh was so swollen that I could not get into the pocket. I promptly passed out. Tony lifted me inside, and gave me a stiff whiskey. Then he drove me home and helped Ena get me settled for what proved my last night at Old Kasenga.

A year later, Tony's sister Marjorie retired from teaching, and came out to do a year of voluntary work in Choma. She was a very conventional and correct English lady. Tony was alarmed, but we so managed things that she returned to England without knowing about the little houses behind Jones's Store.

Alf Palfreyman

Half way between Old Kasenga and Baambwe village stood Alf's little store. Here I always paused for a break in the twenty mile journey. It was a store like no other I had ever seen. Alf catered exclusively for village customers who were perhaps rich in cattle, but possessed little cash. He sold many of the things stocked in big grocery stores, but they were packed into very small packets and portions; a screw of ten matches, a tiny tin of condensed milk or coffee, four or five sweets, five cigarettes, patches for punctures in little tins. The only normal containers were the bottles of Fanta orange juice, which I considered the most delicious liquid I had ever tasted, especially after pedalling my heavy bike for twelve miles through deep sand in the burning heat. Alf performed a useful social service. He was sorely missed when he retired, not to his native Yorkshire, but to the sunny Seychelles.

Pearson Likukela

Pearson was in his last year of training at Kafue when we taught there. He stood out from the rest, and we employed him in several little jobs as gardener and baby-sitter so that he could raise funds, since he was an orphan, raised by an uncle. The uncle was a Local Preacher and should have known better, but he used the money that should have paid for Pearson's maintenance to buy himself a new shotgun. During that year we became friends, and when we were posted to Ila country, I invited Pearson to accompany us to help me with the new language. Although Lozi by birth, he had been raised as a Mwila, and spoke the language as his native tongue. Week by week he came round the villages with me and helped my stumbling efforts.

One morning near the start of the rains, we set off early to walk through the bush to Mukobela's big village at Baambwe, to teach and preach. Early in the afternoon we set off to walk 10 miles back to Kasenga. After a short way we found water on the path, the puddles became pools and the pools a lake. The annual flood had started before the rains, with water pouring from the hills.

We struggled on for some time, until we broke out from the trees and could see clearly Kasenga mission, less than two miles away on its island. By this time, however, the water was breast high and getting deeper. I was finding it increasingly difficult to force my legs through the water, and gasped "It's no good, Pearson, I can't go on". We had to turn round and retrace our painful steps through the flooded bush. Pearson was a big strong man, and half-carried me until at last we reached the Namwala guest-house, an open shelter by the road, where we spent a damp night. I would never have made it without him. Next day we cadged a lift home from Namwala via the main road, a distance of twenty-five miles.

After a month or two, Pearson went back to Kafue to take up his teaching job, and I lost touch with him. Thirty years later, Ena and I were helping the grand-daughter of an old friend, who had gone to study the Bible at a college in South Africa. She wrote to tell us that one of her fellow students was an old acquaintance of ours. His name was Pearson.

Pearson

It so happened that I had embarked on writing my dictionary of Ila usage, and was running into difficulties with idiomatic and obsolete words and phrases. Pearson offered to help, and I soon realised that he was not just an Ila speaker, but an accomplished linguist and scholar with a flair for analysis and research. Soon I was posting him a weekly list of puzzles to decipher, and he returned them with detailed explanations and parsing. We phoned each other often, and he invariably greeted me with "Praise the Lord!", in a full rich baritone.

The dictionary numbered over nine hundred pages, and took several years to complete. I wrote in the preface "The dictionary could never have been completed without continual reference to a linguist having Ila as his first language, and I have relied heavily on Mr Pearson Kahwema Likukela, of Kabwe, Zambia. Mr Likukela was raised at Namwala, and has a wide knowledge of Ila in all its dialects and branches. His zeal for the Ila language and his constant readiness to give his time freely over the last three years and in the midst of a busy life have saved me from embarrassing howlers and awkward gaps. He has illuminated many an obscure phrase and translated many an obsolete word, and I owe him a profound debt".

When Pearson graduated from Bible college, we were able to send him a splendid gown which we came across at Oxfam, and when he retired from teaching a year or two later, he got a little house. Unfortunately he did not live to enjoy it. I still miss his deep voice opening his weekly phone call in a rich baritone, "Praise the Lord!"

Dorothy Nabanyama

Dorothy was one of girl twins, born near Maala before the first world war. At that period the Baila regarded such a birth as ill-omened, and their mother would be required to expose them to die. This she would do by letting them slip from a sling on her back into an ant-bear hole or into a river, unseen.

Dorothy and her sister were the first two such twins to survive, as they had been rescued and raised by John Price, the missionary at Kasenga. Dorothy married Johanne Nabanyama, who became a greatly respected local Preacher, and her sister married Matthew Lucheya, the first and only African Chairman of the Methodist Church.

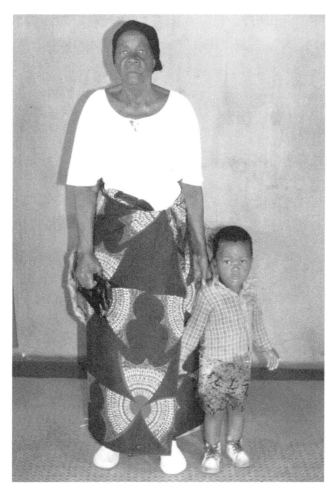

Mrs Nabanyama

When we first arrived at Kasenga, Dorothy was widowed, and leader of the local Red Blouse sisterhood, who were dedicated to a strict code of Christian conduct. Ena continues…

"One day they reproached me – very gently – for drinking alcohol. I said, "Jesus drank." They must have found this acceptable, as they allowed me to remain a member of the group. I reflected with amusement that I was supposed to be preaching to them, not the other way round. Was this success or failure?"

The only alcohol known to the Red Blouses was that of the village beer-drinks. These often lasted for days, resulting in total insensibility, after

The Red Blouse Sisterhood

drunken dancing and sex. When Dennis went for the first time to introduce himself to Chief Mukobela at his great village at Baambwe, ten miles away, the chief was embarrassed because most of his people were lying about recovering from a lengthy binge. "Come next week", he suggested. "They will have recovered by then." When I did so, Mukobela sent round his official messengers, who soon assembled a sober congregation of several hundred for me.

Dorothy was a good friend, and highly thought of. During the interregnum following our return to England, Kasenga Girls' School fell on hard times, and the Government salaries were sometimes well in arrears. Dorothy was called in to help, rather than the official person in charge, and became in effect a school governor.

For thirty years she wrote a weekly letter to us in England, which not only kept us abreast of affairs, but also kept my command of the language fresh, since she always wrote in idiomatic Ila. Her strong Christian faith was most impressive. When she suspected that one of her relations had poisoned a close member of her family, she wrote that she was not going to seek vengeance, but would leave that to God.

Shortly before her death, she suggested that I write a book about Kasenga, and it was this which led to me producing the Dictionary of Ila Usage and the subsequent books for the African Institute and Kew.

SNAKES

*I*n the wet season the Kafue River flooded, and Kasenga became a snake sanctuary for the Kafue Flats, as snakes of every shape and size hurried for refuge with us. We never looked at the view when we went for a walk – just at the ground ahead. Ena continues…

"A year after we first arrived at Kafue Training Institute, even before we went to Kasenga, I had an encounter with a boomslang. It was dangling in a tree close by. Feeling suave and knowledgeable, after a whole year in Africa, I threw a stone at it. I was appalled to see it 'fly' from its tree to another tree some yards away.

I was taking young Rebecca for a walk one day. She was trotting a few yards ahead, when we saw a cobra in the path about twelve feet in front of her, risen and ready to strike. I whispered 'Rebecca! Snake! Come back, slowly!' Rebecca did exactly as she was told without arguing. She must have heard the fear in my voice. It was a narrow escape.

On another occasion, I had ventured along a path, near the house but unfamiliar to me. Suddenly I saw part of a huge snake about six yards ahead. Its head and tail were hidden on either side of the path. What happened next was like something out of a film. I must have picked up Rebecca and fled, but I remember nothing except being back at the house. It must have been a python. I never explored that path again".

Black Mambas were deadly, and could outpace a running man. The road up to the church at Nanzhila was closed to pedestrian traffic for over a year because of one which killed several travellers.

One morning at New Kasenga, a girl reported to me that a mamba had reared up in the path just in front of a file of girls walking from the dormitory into class. It had then disappeared into a big tree by the path, and the girls were in a ring round the tree watching out for it. I grabbed a gun and piled a bonfire round the trunk. Soon smoke was pouring up into the tree, while I waited with gun ready. Alas, at that point the heavens opened and torrents of rain put us all to flight. The snake was never seen again.

I was once unloading a load of brushwood from the back of the Land Rover, when a twig in my grasp writhed into life. I hurled it out and way, and saw a deadly boomslang *(Dispholidus typus typus)* shoot off.

One evening at New Kasenga, Ena was shutting our chickens into their snake-proof house for the night. We kept them in the top half of a corrugated aluminium water tank, which was planted into the sand, and sealed by a close-fitting drop-door. She shone her lamp in to check them, when she saw one gradually disappearing down the open jaws of a large snake. I came out with a rifle, and peered in while Ena held the torch. For thirty minutes we tried to get the snake, and I fired at shadows several times. In the end, after trying in vain to make all secure, we realised that the snakes treated our henhouse as a snack bar, and we gave up trying to keep chickens at New Kasenga.

A year or two later, in broad daylight, I saw from my office window an enormous python making its way across the short grass in front. I had a rifle handy and shot it. I was intrigued to find two neat claws on the rear part of its body. We found its stomach filled with eggs. The skin was twelve feet long, and I took it back to England and kept it displayed on the wall until it got maggoty.

LEOPARDS AND
LEOPARD WOMEN

The first leopard I saw was at Kafue. The Mission calves were locked in a solid shed at night, with a six-inch ventilation gap between the top of the door and the brickwork. One night there was a great commotion, and I discovered that a calf had been taken. Daylight revealed blood and hairs on the top of the locked door. The trail of blood was not hard to follow, and it led to a tree about a hundred yards away. The leopard had climbed a tree, carrying the calf in its jaws, and was up there in a fork, coolly eating its prey. We did not want to spoil its hide with a shot gun, so Japhet, our foreman, shot it with a rifle, and took the nine-foot pelt as his trophy.

I am still astounded, fifty-four years later, when I reflect on the power and agility needed to scramble six feet up a sheer door, squeeze through a six inch gap, kill a calf as big as itself, squeeze back through the gap, and climb a tree with it.

One evening I was driving home from Namwala with medicines when I had to stop sharply. A leopard followed by two cubs emerged from the bush on the right, and crossed the road to the left. She turned and looked at me, but neither hurried nor slowed her stately pace. I was mesmerised by the beauty of the stately procession.

The third leopard measured nine feet from nose to tail. Short, our wood cutter, brought it to show us one morning. He explained that he had heard a commotion in his cattle kraal on the Mission during the night, so he had pushed in amongst the panic-stricken beasts, and killed the leopard with his spear as it was biting one of them. Short was as small as his name, yet he modestly related the story as an everyday incident.

Short, the leopard killer

"Leopard woman" was the nearest our younger son could get to "leper woman". One little woman used to come each week for Ena to rub her scalp with meths, to kill the irritating lice. She lacked hands, so could not rub her own head. She was a nice old lady, and we got to know her well. One day, she arrived in great distress, and told us that she was being expelled from her village as a useless mouth. We got a little house made for her at the back of our garden; only daub and wattle, with a thatched roof, but it was her retirement home, and she was happy there with our family and plenty of visitors to chat with. At that time we thought that leprosy could not be caught by touch. Later we heard that it could, which gave us rather a shock. Ena remembers the red-letter day when the Surveyor's helicopter landed nearby. She was carrying baby Jack, and the old lady had no toes, so they tottered along together as best they could to see the marvel. I was away at a distant village, and missed all the excitement.

When the 'Leopard' woman died, her place in our garden was soon filled by another, but I remember nothing of her.

JAMESON

One Sunday I was taking morning service in New Kasenga church. Ena was in the middle of the church at the back with Rebecca and Stephen, aged five and four, on either side. The door opened noisily and in stalked a strange figure, with wild hair, staring eyes, and wrists fettered to a plough chain thrown over his shoulder. Ena moved Stephen to her other side for safety, and the service continued with barely a ripple.

After the service, the girls told us that he was a madman living in a nearby village. The people of the village had to chain him to the centre-post of a house whenever he became violent, which happened regularly. We took him back to the house. He could not speak, but showed by signs that he had come to have his wrists dressed, as they were chafed raw by the fetters. I took off the chain, Ena dressed and bandaged his wounds, and he went off to the village.

On the following Saturday evening, there was a banging on our front door, which had a glass panel. I took a lamp to investigate, and saw the madman's face pressed against the glass, eyes staring desperately. We let him in and found him in a sorry state. He was practically naked and trussed with wire from shoulder to thigh. We freed him, dressed his injuries, gave him an old shirt, and bedded him down in my office. Next day I took him to the doctor at Choma. "What do you think this is, a bloody loony bin?" he asked, as he threw us out.

I drove him the hundred miles back to Namwala, where the DC put him in gaol for a week. For the next six weeks the poor man was passed round like a parcel between me, the Namwala DC, and his home village. Finally one of his legs got broken, and I managed to persuade the Clerk of the Court at Choma to certify him for his own safety, and he was at last taken to a mental ward at Lusaka. That, we thought, was the end of our involvement.

We were wrong. Several months later, a stranger called on us. He was a fine, well-built young man, in well pressed khaki drill and splendid brown boots. "You are my father and mother", he informed us. He told us how he was our poor lunatic, who had been cured in the hospital by a young specialist from Bolton called Alan Haworth. It turned out that his illness was physical, caused by pressure on his brain when the moon was full. It was cured by drugs, and a new life had begun for him. In the absence of any family except for one brother, he looked to us instead, and for years Jameson Mukasyingu sent letters to us from Zambia, and we supplied him with parcels of (slightly worn) clothes and shoes. After a few years, he told us of his coming marriage, and we heard no more. The young doctor, Alan Howarth, went on to a distinguished international career.

GUNS

We took out from England a .38 Webley revolver and a beautiful Westley-Richards Express rifle, which had belonged to the Duke of Bolton. Northern Rhodesia in the 'fifties was a violent society. Firearms, from automatic rifles to pocket pistols, were freely on sale to Europeans. Several of the mission stations we served in had weapons in the inventory. There was a whole armoury at Old Kasenga; at Lusaka manse the inventory included an automatic rifle, which had no pretence of being a sporting weapon. I handed it in to the police.

It soon became obvious even to me that our own rifle, for which each round cost several pounds, was an extravagance. The limit was reached one day when I was required to butcher one of the mission cattle to provide meat for the school, as the floods had prevented delivery of the butcher's meat. I shot a fat cow behind the shoulder, but the round passed right through, and it stood fast. I put a round through its brain, but it merely shook its head. I finally dropped it by putting the muzzle of my revolver against its forehead. The bullets had cost the price of a whole carcass. The final blow came when it was butchered and found to be in calf, so we also lost the price of two new cattle. At least we did not lose the rifle. I sold it to Charlie Lamuniere for £50, the sum it cost me, and the money paid for Ena and me to have a week's holiday in the Victoria Falls Hotel, while Charlie charged off to shoot buffalos.

Late one night at Kasenga, when I was away on tour and Ena was alone with three small children, she was awakened by hammering at the door and the sound of drunken voices. It was a time of great unrest with refugees coming in from the Congo. She got the revolver out of the drawer and tried to load it from a box of cartridges. Fortunately, she was unable to break it open to do so, and had to open the door armed only by prayer. Her lantern revealed a group of drunk and merry men, who explained that they had run out of petrol and pushed their van to our house in the hope of getting some from us. "Certainly, certainly!" she replied. They filled up from our 45-gallon drum in the yard, and drove off with cheers and thanks. Next day they returned with a magnificent bunch of plantains.

Not all gun stories had happy endings, however. In 1959 the students at Kafue went on strike about their food, and refused to leave the dormitory and go to their lessons. It was still a time of great political unrest, and the new head over-reacted and called the police. An armoured car rolled up, and when the pupils refused to budge from the dormitory, several rounds of .5 machine gun bullets were fired through the top of the walls.

The whole student body was expelled and replaced by a new intake. Several dozen young lives had been blighted by one mistake. The whole episode was quickly expunged from the records, and Philip Pearson's book on the 'History of the Kafue Training Institute' makes no mention of it.

Another instance occurred in 1964. The newly independent government of Kenneth Kaunda faced an emergency in Chinsali province, up in the north-east. The followers of the prophetess Alice Lenshina rebelled against the authorities and the ruling UNIP party, and were

Kafue dormitories

ruthlessly suppressed by four platoons of soldiers. Many of her followers were shot and tortured. Estimates of the deaths varied wildly, and thousands of Lumpa adherents fled to the Congo.

John Hannaford was DC there at the time, and wrote to me "Life here has been a little hectic during the past ten days. The incident at Kamello village resulted in five deaths and six injured – two very badly." When next we met, he described the appalling scene he found in the big Lumpa church building, where the rebels had made their last stand. Bloodstains reached high up on the walls. One can only imagine the world outcry if this had taken place a month or two earlier, while the British were still in control. As it was, the whole affair was hushed up, and only recently has an agitation for the impeachment of Kenneth Kaunda for genocide been set afoot.

THE LONG AND THE
SHORT AND THE TALL

The old World War I song fitted Methodist missionaries as well as soldiers; they certainly came in all shapes and sizes. They were not set apart by excessive spirituality or asceticism, and displayed a wide range of behaviour in their response to exile. At the top of the list in our experience were the nurses and the nuns.

Connie Howard

Connie was one of the most remarkable missionaries we met. She was the mission nurse at Kafue clinic when we worked at the school there. Ena was pregnant with our second child, and woke me up early one morning to say that her waters had broken, and she had to get to Kafue hospital urgently. I rushed over to ask Winston Jubb, the Principal, to take us there in the Mission car, as I had no licence then.

Ena relates the story: "Winston nobly assented, but added insouciantly that he would just finish his breakfast first. By the time he had finished, my pregnancy was even further advanced, so Winston asked Connie to go with us. She must have instilled in him some sense of urgency, as we set off at a mighty lick along the rough road, demolishing an ant-bear en route. It was possibly at this point that Winston yelled 'Shall we stop?' Connie and I shouted with one voice 'No, don't stop!' alarming him still further. We had seven miles to cover, and my whole labour was completed in the car, with Connie attending to me in the back seat and Winston driving like Stirling Moss. As we approached the emergency entrance, Connie said 'Whatever you do, don't push!' Ten minutes later, I gave birth to a bouncing baby boy, and Connie and I became lifelong friends".

Connie had her fiftieth birthday soon after our arrival at Kafue, and was touched when Ena made her a cake to celebrate. She was lean and sinewy, deeply tanned with neat grey hair. Not conventionally pretty, she had large expressive eyes and a radiant smile. Nothing fazed her. Her equipment in the clinic was basic. I remember vividly how she had to sterilise and re-use hypodermic needles, even after they lost their pristine acuity, because I experienced them in my own arm on occasion.

Connie with Becky at Old Kasenga church

Yet she carried out emergency operations which in England would have required a team of surgeons. One of our senior Local Preachers was cycling along a bush road, with his four-year-old daughter riding on the crossbar. A leopard attacked them. The preacher was a powerful man, and managed to kill the beast after a desperate struggle which left him disembowelled and grievously wounded. He stuffed his entrails back before fainting, and a car came and got him to Connie's clinic. She stitched him together and dressed his wounds, before taking him to the hospital at Kafue. He recovered, but his little girl's body was never found.

Years before our arrival in Zambia, Connie had suffered a breakdown through overwork at the hospital at Kasenga, and had been told never to return there. Nevertheless, she came to stay with us for a holiday there because of our friendship. When in 1983 we told her that we were going to take over a children's home in Nazareth, she volunteered to come and help. She was 74 and matron of Kingswood School, so her offer had to be turned down, much to our regret.

Cecil Hopgood

Cecil, The Authority on the Tonga language, was well loved as a "character". On his first rail journey north from Capetown, he found that he had lost his wallet, containing all his money. A lesser man would have made a great fuss, but not Cecil. When he changed trains at Bulawayo, three days later, he was met by a local Methodist lady, who took him home for tea. Her surprise turned into amazement, as Cecil gratefully consumed vast quantities of sandwiches and cakes, and revealed that he had not eaten for three days.

At one Synod I saw the taciturn linguist take a hammer and bash a sheet of paper right through the panel of the wooden door, because he did not agree with what was written on it. I sympathised, but lacked the confidence to do the same. Later I noticed that there was a small snake coiled on the floor under his chair. When I pointed this out, he merely remarked "I know" and went on reading. Later, when we entertained him for a meal, we found him perfectly agreeable and well mannered.

Other colleagues

One synod I kept getting funny looks, and realised that people were talking about me. Finally, a friend told me that a fellow worker was going round telling everybody at the Synod that I was a hopeless dipsomaniac. When I sought him out indignantly, he explained that he had recently fallen from a plane at 30,000 feet, and landed on his head, so could take no responsibility for his actions. He was sent home for treatment.

Another colleague had no such excuse for traducing us. On first arriving in the country, he was sent to Lusaka for me to introduce him to the work. I was taking him by bicycle round Matero, the largest African township, when I heard a crash and angry shouting behind me.

I turned back, and saw him on the ground in a tangle of bicycles and people. A fast-growing crowd was busy abusing and kicking him. I pushed into the crowd, and yelled out in Ila that we were missionaries and not colonialist oppressors. By a miracle, many in the crowd were Ila people, and they backed off, allowing us to ride away.

It appeared that my companion had collided with a bicycle which had emerged without warning from a side street. On the bicycle were a man, his wife and two children, in a wobbly pyramid. The collision was spectacular.

My smug satisfaction at saving him soon evaporated, however. Far from feeling gratitude for his deliverance, the young man promptly sent home a newsletter, of which copies were carelessly left on the office desk. I was astonished to read that Ena and I were, in fact, typical colonialists and racialists.

The young man and his wife spent only a year in the country, and never ventured into rural mission work. On their return to England, they had successful careers as experts on Central African church matters.

EXILES AND WIDOWERS

*W*hen children grew to school age, missionary wives had two options: to take them back to school in England, or to teach them by means of the government correspondence courses from Salisbury. Ena chose the latter option, but many mothers chose to go back to England. This often resulted in discreet liaisons on the part of the "grass widowers", regrettable but venial. There was nothing venial or discreet, however, about one man who openly set up a ménage-a-trois with his wife and an au-pair girl.

Others turned out to be round pegs in square holes. The couple whom we replaced at Old Kasenga realised on arrival that the place was not for them. They headed straight back without unpacking, leaving us to arrange for their boxes to be returned to the line-of-rail. Afterwards they worked very successfully in a different area.

TRAVEL

*K*asenga circuit was roughly the size of Wales, so getting round it occupied much of my time. In the rainy season it became an island, and we had to propel dugout canoes to reach the mainland. Since a canoe was hacked and burned out of a section of eucalyptus tree, it was unsinkable. It was, however, prone to capsize when the pole stuck in the mud. Once I was returning from the bank at Choma with a month's salary for all our primary teachers. They were paid in half-crowns, so the wages box was large and heavy. I capsized in two feet of water and six inches of mud. It was several hours before I managed to recover the last coin.

On another occasion, I was standing on the Maala side of the floods, waiting for Wilmot Munyimba, my young assistant minister, to bring our

Our canoes

dugout canoe across from Kasenga. I watched as he poled the canoe over the half-mile of water. Suddenly his tempo speeded up dramatically, and he covered the last few hundred yards in what was surely world-record time. When he reached me and clambered out, his normal cheerful black face was nearly as pale as mine, and he could hardly speak for a minute or two. "Dennis", he stammered, "you must get me a shotgun licence before I go in that canoe again. I was being chased by a crocodile all the way!" Soon he had a new Greener 12-bore shotgun, loaded with ball.

Sikolete, our faithful cook, was not so fortunate. He sometimes went out in a canoe at night with a lantern to fish, but one night he didn't come back. We found the remains of the canoe, which had been bitten in half by hippo. His body was never found.

On short journeys up to twenty miles we cycled or walked. For longer journeys, Ena bought me a Honda motor-bike. This was a revelation. Honda had just started operating in Zambia, and their new bikes weighed little more than our old unwieldy pushbikes, and would tackle any sand, slope, mud or distance.

The Honda

For carrying loads, we had a Land Rover. It had a starting handle, and if the windscreen wiper stopped, you could turn it by a knob above the dashboard. It had lots of extra gears to get you through mud. It did not matter that it only did ten miles to the gallon, because petrol was so cheap. It would stand any amount of overloading and abuse. However, the great thing about it was its simplicity – it was a true DIY vehicle. At various times, I had to fashion a rear spring from a branch, a main engine gasket from a 100lb sugar-bag, a seal for a leaking radiator with porridge and a broken fan belt with tights, in order to drive the hundred miles to the garage for repairs.

One day Mary Lawrence and Olive Wilks, two of our teachers at New Kasenga, drove to Choma to catch the train. They took John Ndemena, one of our senior Local Preachers, who had never visited the line-of-rail in his life. On the way, Mary turned over the Land Rover. Olive was only shaken, and able to catch her train next day, but Mary broke her shoulder, and needed plastic surgery on her face. John never did get to Choma, and the Land Rover was out of action for over four months. When we got it back eventually, its steering was never the same, and I sold it for £200. The chap who bought it killed himself in it shortly afterwards.

Our next vehicle was a long-wheelbase Land Rover, kindly supplied by Oxfam. I soon spoiled its pristine appearance by hitting a large kudu bull at speed, but we were able to get it repaired.

The roads were hazardous in all seasons. Even the main road to Lusaka was single-track, with two concrete strips laid directly on the sand. When two cars met, each had to move away from the strips, over to the near side, raising enormous clouds of dust. In the wet, the cars slithered through the mud. It was a point of honour not to slacken speed. The scariest trip of my

Oxfam's Landrover with elephants

Testing the road to Old Kasenga

life was when Bob Toland, a friend from Choma, kindly gave me a lift home from Lusaka. He had just taken delivery of an enormous Chevrolet saloon which he told me would reach 100mph. This he proceeded to demonstrate for the whole of the way home.

Some stretches of road were dead straight for mile after mile. This monotony posed its own dangers, as it was only too easy to drowse and run off the road. I used to take strong snuff to keep awake.

The side roads were intercepted by numerous low bridges over the many streams. In the rains, the streams became raging torrents, bearing all manner of debris. The bridges had no side rails, which would have trapped debris, so there were therefore no precise aiming points to help when crossing the narrow submerged strips. This led to my undoing on the road to Masuku Mission, when I misjudged the centre and was swept into the flood. I was driving a VW Combi that day, from which I managed to escape and reach the bank. Only the canvas top was visible, like a submerged reef.

It took some hours for me to reach a village and organise a team of oxen. When at last the VW was hauled out on to the bank, and all the water had drained off, I got in and turned the key. The engine started first kick, and I drove on to the Mission unscathed.

That was the only good thing about those later Combis, which were

The bridge on the road to Masuku

produced in a new factory in Southern Rhodesia, with unfortunate results. The petrol tanks were now made from thinner steel, and as they were under the chassis, with no protection from the road, they soon became pitted by the sand and stones thrown up, and leaked. We bought no more VWs, and I was charged by the Synod to examine all the possible replacements on sale in Zambia while waiting in Lusaka for Ena to produce our son Jack. I chose the new Peugeot 404 pickups, which were built like tanks. Unfortunately, the controls were all on the steering column, and I had neglected to familiarise myself with the handbook. I was proudly driving the new car home for the first time, and along a long straight I foolishly decided to test its capabilities. The old Land Rovers and VWs would work up to 60 mph if pushed, but this Peugeot was a different animal, and I was soon touching 80. The powerful headlights picked out a group of people walking along the road in the distance. I started to dip the lights out of courtesy. To my horror I pressed the wrong switch, and the lights went off. All I could do was pray and brake and try to drive straight. When I finally got lights on again, I was in the middle of the group, but had touched none of them.

CALL THE MIDWIFE

*I*n October 1964 Ena was pregnant with our fourth child, the third, Jack, having been born three years earlier in Lusaka. When the baby's head unexpectedly engaged, we went to consult the Sisters of Charity at Namwala, thirty miles to the west. They welcomed us with their usual kindness, and Sister Bernadette told us that the birth could be imminent, that complications were possible, and that we should aim with all speed for Lusaka, where there was a teaching hospital.

That was all very well, but we were over 300 miles from Lusaka, and the roads were primitive. Fortunately it was the dry season, so there would be no floods to contend with. We hastened back to Kasenga. While Ena packed, I worked out our itinerary. There were half a dozen clinics and small hospitals en route, and I charted the distance between each.

We set off with me driving, our Doberman Jessie in the front seat, and Ena with three children in the back. We invented a game for the children. Up to the halfway point to the first little hospital at Macha, the children were to shout 'Point of no return!" We repeated the same process for the other stages. Everybody had a jolly time – except Ena.

At last, we got safely to Lusaka Teaching Hospital. Ena was informed that although the birth was near, it was still a few days off.

We threw ourselves on the hospitality of Rachel Fielder, wife of the Lusaka missionary. After a week, I had to return to my work at Kasenga. News of the happy event was conveyed to me two weeks later, via radio to the District Commissioner at Namwala, who sent out a Kapaso (district messenger) to Kasenga.

Our daughter Sarah was safely delivered by an American and an English doctor by means of the ventouse method, the first time that it had ever been used in Zambia. She would not have survived had we had to go to any of the other clinics *en route*.

Ena later told me that Jessie had been sick on the Fielder's carpet.

NAME THIS CHILD

The Ila people had a strong moral code, which was by no means identical with ours. Theft was discouraged by branding a culprit forehead with "M" for Muteu (thief). Our house at Kasenga had no locks. We had to leave it empty for two weeks each year, when we went to the annual Synod. Not so much as a spoon was ever stolen.

However, the Ila people had a great gift for improvisation, which Europeans thought of as lying. Resourceful improvisers were greatly admired. I first encountered this trait when a man and his young wife came begging for transport to Namwala clinic, as she was overdue with her baby.

Faulah's father

I dropped everything, drove them to Namwala, and left them at the clinic. Next time I was in Namwala, I enquired of Sister Bernadette how things had gone, and found that the woman was not pregnant at all. They had used me as a free taxi to a big beer-drink near Namwala.

Some months later, I was asked by another couple to take them to Namwala clinic. I refused. Later that night the couple returned, begging for help. It was a filthy black night, pouring with rain, but this time I realised that they were clearly distressed, and so I set off with them.

Half way there they hammered on the back of the cab, and said that the baby was coming. We got the wife out on the road, and I delivered the baby in the rain by the light of my headlights, tying the cord with a bit of dirty string and cutting it with my penknife. At the clinic, they put mother and baby to bed and said all was well with them.

A little later they came to show me their baby boy, and told me that they were going to call him "Faulah" after me, the midwife.

BURYING BLUNDERS

Syakalima Munsi, one of our oldest headmen, died in Choma hospital, and I brought home his body for burial.

Ila burial involved excavating at the edge of the village a square pit, the size of a small room. Here the corpse was installed on a chair, with his favourite pipe and axe at his side. The grave was roofed over with timber and turf, so that the dead man was able to continue sharing in the life of the village.

For this reason, Syakalima Munsi could not be laid out in a coffin for his last journey, but had to be seated in his chair to stiffen. I collected him from the morgue, and installed him in the back of my Land Rover, with a wife on either side to support him. The journey back was long and arduous, and by the time I finally reached the Mission, I had completely forgotten what I was carrying in the back. The children dashed out in excitement to welcome me, and see what presents I had brought them from the store. I unlaced the canvas and threw open the back. The wives instantly resumed their loud wailing, and Syakalima Munsi stared out with goggle eyes and a ghastly smile.

Sometime later, I took a sick man to hospital at Choma, where he died. The man was poor, and a stranger to me, so I collected his body from the hospital morgue, and buried him in a plain coffin in Choma Cemetery, where I was the only mourner. I had to deal with various jobs in the garage and the stores, and was at last about to set off home, when I was arrested by the local police for body-snatching.

It turned out that the mortuary attendants had given me the wrong corpse, and when the grieving family came to bury their parent they found a stranger. The attendants swiftly passed the blame to me. I had to get an exhumation order from the magistrate to extract the body which I had buried, and get it duly identified. After a second burial service, it was very late when I finally got home that night.

RABIES

Tony Dawdey, the District Commissioner at Choma, had promised us a Doberman puppy, and I drove to Choma one day to collect it. His house had a longish drive from the gate, and in the open porch was lying a large black bitch, with half-a-dozen puppies frolicking around her. Nobody answered the door, so I pushed a note through to say that I had collected my puppy. Then I examined the noisy active group. We had never owned a dog, and I had no idea how to pick one out. The problem was solved when one of them waddled over to me and piddled on my sandals. I lifted her carefully and took her into my jacket. Then I left, closing the gate behind me. Throughout these proceedings the puppies' mother observed me closely, but without protest, merely snuffling at the back of my bare legs all the way down the drive.

Tony called on us during his next tour a week or two later, intrigued to learn how I had managed to steal one of his Doberman's cherished brood and get out alive. The answer was simple: total ignorance of the deadly peril I had courted. I had no idea what a Doberman was, and she must have been equally at a loss how to deal with such an innocent as me.

The Vet advised us to feed the puppy on ground beef leg-bones and boiled lights, and on this diet she rapidly grew into a beautiful creature, with the elegance and power of a thoroughbred racehorse. She also revealed a sense of humour. When taken out for her daily walk on the veldt, she would run ahead for 100 yards, then turn and charge like an express train, straight at Ena, who would stand very still with a toddler held firmly on either side. At the last second she would swerve like a wing three-quarter, without indicating to which side.

She often exploited this acting ability to deceive us. When we travelled far by Land Rover we always started as a normal family, with me driving,

Ena sitting in front with the smaller toddler Stephen on her knee, and Jessie on the back seat with three-year old Rebecca and the luggage. Before long, Ena would be holding Jessie on her knees in front, with both children in the rear with the baggage, Jessie having produced the most alarming symptoms of imminent sickness with violent heavings and gulps. She had to have her head right out of the open window, or else!

Then Jessie sickened with something. We were alarmed. Rabies was endemic in Zambia, and every dog had to wear a metal tag on its collar to show it had been vaccinated and found free from rabies. Collarless dogs were rounded up annually and strung up to a branch by a back leg, before being dispatched by the vet. This always caused great excitement in the whole area, and the Mission staff turned out in force to help. Nobody grudged the efforts, because we had neighbours who had died of rabies. Every time I visited the villages of my area and was surrounded by a pack of scrawny barking leaping dogs, the danger was at the back of my mind.

One day in October '63, at the height of the hot season, our mission was overrun by a pack of village dogs, which attacked our own dogs. I shot one and sent the head to the vet at Choma, and caught another alive, for observation. Fortunately they were found not to be rabid. However, we knew that the whole sixth form at Choma school had recently been subjected to a course of painful injections round the navel every day for two weeks, because they had dissected a dog which proved to be rabid.

So when our own dog became ill we got the vet straight away. He told us to tie her up for a fortnight. If she lived, the disease would be distemper. If she died, it would be rabies, and our family and staff would have to leave immediately for the hospital at Choma for injections. Those two weeks with the longest we ever lived through. We packed our bags and watched and waited. She did not die. It was distemper.

Our rural existence was abruptly ended when I damaged my thigh in a motor-bike accident. I was strapped on to an iron bed on top of a lorry and left Kasenga for the last time, covered by tearful farewell gifts of chickens, eggs, and maize cobs, bound for Choma hospital.

Our new bungalow at Choma was a large rambling one with each room leading out of another. The front door had a pane of glass, broken by the frantic efforts of next-door's amorous labrador to get at Jessie, and I had nailed plywood over the gap pending the glazier's visit. That same night our bishop arrived on a pastoral tour, and was installed on a low camp bed in my office. I was woken by a crash as the persistent lover battered the plywood of the front door. I took the sjambok to it, but the frenzied dog broke through, pounding round the house after Jessie. She ran to my study and leapt over the bishop's bed, with her lover in close pursuit. I followed closely, whipping the labrador and leaping over the bed in my turn. It was only at this point that the bishop reminded me of his presence by sitting up. Once more, memory fails at this interesting point.

When we finally left Africa, we left Jessie with a farmer friend. He wrote some weeks later to say that Jessie would not eat for days after our departure. It was only their little daughter who managed to coax her out of depression and back to life.

EDUCATION

There were two main differences between schooling in Zambia and that in the UK. In Zambia there were no free schools, and there were no reluctant or uninterested pupils. Because schools were built and run by Missions, all the pupils had to pay fees to cover the costs; yet in spite of this, youngsters eagerly competed for places. At Kasenga Girls' School, the fees were £250 per year, including food and two uniforms.

At Kafue Training Institute, boys walked great distances to get places. When every place had been filled, several hopefuls built themselves huts, and waited for incumbents to die, although they were only young teenagers. One of my tasks as acting Head was to stop the boys from working too hard. I used to go round the dormitories after dark, to make spot checks and stop them from working by torchlight under the blankets.

Kasenga Girls' School was one of the few schools of its kind at that time. Run by Olive Wilks and a committed body of teachers, it provided education up to the equivalent of Standard Six. Hitherto, 12-year olds had been married to elderly polygamists.

Jean Hill was a particularly gifted VSO who came for a year to teach at the school. She gathered many revealing details. One of her most promising pupils, Sarah Chanaika, did not return after Christmas break because she had been married off to a man "with sheets on his bed".

Jean arranged English pen-friends for some of the girls. They were horrified to learn that their pen-friends travelled under the ground in London, and begged them not to do so, as they might have been buried alive.

When the girls came back each term, they had to stuff their bug-infested mattresses with clean straw. Their duties covered maintenance of the area, which included cutting the grass. This was by no means the same as mowing the lawn in England. "I came back from Christmas in South Africa", wrote Jean, "and drove past the school because the grass had grown so tall in the weeks I was away… a Bush Baby had taken up residence in my kitchen drawer, and a troop of baboons was roosting in the tree beside my house".

One father told Jean, "My daughter must be educated: I will sell my ducks!" One girl was bitten by a snake while collecting firewood, and two others were delayed by having to drive an elephant out of the mealie field.

A job that the girls hated was dealing with the cesspit, which had to be covered in sand when the effluent overflowed.

They came with zest and freshness to lessons. Only ten of the girls had ever been on a train, so their horizon was limited. *"If I were a princess",* wrote one, in a lesson which Ena gave, *"I should like to have many clothes. I would buy many blankets and big beds. In my house there would be many chairs and tables, different kinds of plates, and cups for me and my family. I should like to have sugar, bread and flour in my house. I would buy two bags of rice. I would spend one pound on sweets and biscuits. I would like apples and oranges, bananas and mangoes to eat. I would give money to the poor people and sick people. If I had children, I would send them to school".*

One day, a headman I knew well came to me in a state of high indignation, showing me his bitten finger. "My daughter Margaret bit me!" he said. "Talk to her! Make her obey me!" Gradually the story came out. He had removed his daughter from the school when she reached twelve, to marry her off. When she objected, he beat her. She bit his finger, so he locked her up. I took the case to Chief Mungaila who sided with Margaret and returned her to school. She went on to become a successful teacher, and after this landmark decision, Ila girls were able to complete their education up to Standard Six at Kasenga.

If the girls lacked sophistication in comparison with English schoolgirls, they were far beyond them in spirituality. They embraced Christianity fervently and joyfully. To my amazement, the first twenty whom I baptised at New Kasenga spent the whole of the previous night at prayer in the church. One of our abiding memories is of Easter at Kasenga, when the girls walked round before dawn, dressed in white, singing the haunting Easter carol:

Jesu Krisitu wabuka, wabuka! (has risen)
Jesu Krisitu wabuka, wabuka!
Jesu Krisitu wabuka, Alleluyah, Alleluyah!
Alleluyah! Alleluyah!

Their faith was fresh and real, like that described in the Acts of the Apostles, and it refreshed us in turn.

PRIVATE EDUCATION
(CARRIED OUT BY ENA)

From the start, Rebecca led the way in our private education. A letter home at this time revealed how Stephen, fifteen months younger than she, extended his vocabulary by repeating every word she said, whether he understood it or not. At the age of five, I enrolled her in a correspondence course sent from South Africa. The two other children did not like to be left out, so I enrolled them privately, according to their abilities.

I am afraid we were a disappointment to the organisers from the start. Rebecca spoilt their pattern, by being a year ahead of her reading age. She passed her exam for Infants II with a gold star, having "Very Good" in everything except handwriting, which was merely "Good". The tutor's response was to put her back a year, with the excuse that her writing was untidy. To make matters worse, Stephen wrote his version on the pages of her question book, instead of on paper. Meanwhile Jack, aged three, sat there trying his best to follow.

We were sent the script of the pantomime "Aladdin", so we decided to produce it in our little model theatre, and gave a tiny part to Jack. When the question "Ave a banana?" was asked, Jack had to reply "Abanazar?" We practised daily. At last his big moment came. Cue: "Ave a banana?" Long silence. He had forgotten it. Ah, well! We praised him immensely all the same.

Another time, we played a new record from England, Fats Waller's "Your feet's too big!" The responses were immediate: Rebecca said "No they're not". Stephen said "How does he know?" Jack said "Which foot?" They were sure they were being personally insulted.

Rebecca's knowledge was a two-edged sword. One of the letters which she wrote to her Daddy while he was in hospital for a few days was as follows:

Dear daddy

I hope you are well. We have got a lot of Xmas cards we went to get some manure to Johns house when we were there those logs ats round the manure she nealy went over them did you go on your motor bike a lot. I hope it will be tidy when you come home. we have got some Sweetys from nana now. I am not dreesd yet.

good by for now.

love from Rebecca.

In another letter she wrote:

Dear Daddy

I hope you are a bit better! Stephen was happy without you. We went round and round this morning and we got dizzy. all the time mummy was at school we scibbed and then coloured it

love from Rebecca −XXX-

Home schooling

CITY SLICKERS

*A*t the beginning of 1961 St. Paul's church at Lusaka was vacated by the sudden decision of the incumbent to emigrate to Australia. Ena was pregnant with our third child. The solution was simple: transfer the Fowler family to St. Paul's for a few months.

We found it a different world. Kasenga had been quiet and peaceful but here the atmosphere was alive with political agitation as the desire for "Lwanguluko" (untying) became ever stronger. As I signed the inventory for our new flat, I was amazed to see that it included an assault rifle, which I hastily deposited in the Boma.

St Paul's was a non-European church in Matero, the big sprawling African township. It bordered the army drill ground, and every morning we could watch the riot squad practising. About a dozen men, each carrying a dustbin lid and a pick axe handle, stood shoulder to shoulder. At the command, they chanted a fierce battle cry and beat the picks against the dustbin lids. Another command, and they advanced for a few yards, as they drove back an invisible crowd.

I was a sort of chaplain to the regiment, and had to address them from time to time. Since they had no common language, I had to speak in English and wait after each sentence until it was translated into Tonga, Nyanja, Bemba and Swahili. It made for short pithy sermons.

I had to teach theology to the sixth form at Munali College, and was appalled to learn that it was the sole sixth form in the whole of Northern Rhodesia, after so many years of British rule.

A more interesting duty was my weekly radio talk. Saucepan radio sets were developed in 1949 by the Ever Ready Company in Britain, and made in large numbers. Their blue disc faces were a familiar sight in towns and villages across the whole country, serving both to inform and unite.

I took over as "Radio Padre", answering questions sent in by listeners. I can remember only one: "Dear Padre, where does the hair of a bald man go? I work as houseboy for a very bald man, but I never see any hair on the floor." Unfortunately I have forgotten my answer.

ONE MAN, ONE VOTE, ONCE

*I*n 1965 the first ever presidential election in Zambia based on universal suffrage was held. The voting station in our area was at Kabulamwanda school, a short distance from our house. Ena and I went to vote, together with Gideon, our cook. The two candidates were Kenneth Kaunda, leader of the United National Independence Party, based in Lusaka, and Harry Nkumbula, born in Maala, and the pioneer for many years of the campaign for "Lwanguluko". Harry was hot favourite here in his home area, but we preferred his opponent. We queued in the crowd at the front door, until the clerk came out, and beckoned Ena and me to go inside. There we cast our votes for UNIP.

We noticed that our papers were handed in at the table where the votes were being counted. The supervisor read them, and called us over. "Don't leave by the front door," he told us. We thought this rather odd, but obeyed. We climbed out of the back window, and made our way safely home by a circuitous route. Gideon, our cook, was not so lucky. He was chased through the bush for hours by ANC supporters, before managing to get back to us.

ONE-DAY WONDERS

*E*verybody knows that clergy lead an easy life, and work a one-day week. Missionary clergy are even less well regarded. When we returned from Africa in 1966, the local press reporter interviewed us. We were taken aback to read the resulting article. It appeared that we had been living a life of luxury in a tropical paradise, ministered to by an enormous staff, whom we exploited by paying slave wages. We had brought back with us no fewer than 36 boxes, laden with our spoils.

In fact, the 36 boxes contained our total worldly possessions after 11 years of marriage. Many were filled with books. It was indeed true that we employed a staff of nine: a herdsman, a wood-cutter, a gardener, a cook, a houseboy, a nurse, and a nanny. We needed them because Ena was working an average 70-hour week, teaching our children by correspondence course from Salisbury, treating scores of patients, running sewing classes at three villages, obtaining second-hand clothes from England and organising sales to raise cash for medicines for her dispensary, teaching French in the school, and giving hospitality to the constant flow of visitors.

Alimon Mwandwe, the herdsman, had the care of our cows and oxen. He slept in a loft above the cattle, and had two vital tasks: to bring us our daily water ration from the river, and to take the water drum from the chassis, and replace it by a cart body, whenever we ourselves needed to be hauled across the floodplain.

Short, our woodcutter, was occupied fulltime in getting fuel for our cooking stove and boiler, often going deep into the bush to find suitable branches. (Incidentally, many of the names by which the servants were known to us sound quaint and naive. Ila culture prescribed strict rules for personal names. It was forbidden to speak one's own real name, or the name of one's father or mother or sister-in-law. A husband could not use his wife's name, nor she use her husband's. They could not even use words that sounded like names. A father had to refer to his son as *"Muselyata"*, "My father's namesake". The word *"kusontomoka"* means both to use a name wrongly, and to fall flat on one's face. Hence the use of silly names like Short, Cigarette, Margarine, Shilling, etc.)

The gardener tended the little garden, our only source of fruit and vegetables. This entailed digging a complicated system of irrigation channels to take the used water in the bath to the plants. He also dug deep refuse pits for disposal of our kitchen waste, and made new pits as needed.

Rhoda Shileu, the nurse, was employed part-time in Ena's dispensary, her wages paid from the proceeds of Ena's auctions and teaching.

Maudie the nanny followed the children round, to stop them getting lost in the Bush or running into danger. She was sacked when we found her at the well with our three young children, giving each in turn a bunk up to look over the parapet into the depths.

Our houseboy cleaned the house, and washed our clothing and the nappies. After handing them out to dry, he had to iron every article to kill the jiggers and putzi eggs. The irons were big iron ones, filled with charcoal. He stayed with us for some years, until he was killed by a hippo while fishing at night.

White, our cook, made perfect meals from very limited resources, and never took more than 5% of our stores as his perk. He was succeeded by Gideon, who was equally accomplished.

We had to work very long hours, because there were so many jobs that had to be done before we could get down to our religious work. We lived in the most unhealthy region of Northern Rhodesia, with young children, 120 hard miles from the nearest English hospital, 65 miles from the American doctor at Macha Mission, and 25 miles from the nuns' clinic at Namwala. Organising treatment for our frequent illnesses and accidents took much time and effort.

For example, after a week-long break at Victoria Falls, we spent all Friday driving home over muddy roads. On Saturday, Stephen developed an abscess and a temperature of 104 degrees. On Sunday, I had to drive him to the doctor at Macha, which involved a boat crossing. The doctor lanced the boil and injected penicillin, and after lunch we drove home, arriving very late and exhausted.

The maintenance of our boat took hours. When the floods ended in

May, the boat was sunk in shallow water. When the rains returned, the boat was lifted and dried out, and all the seams caulked with boiling pitch. Finally, it was sanded and repainted.

We lived far from the nearest garage. This presented a problem which took many hours of hard labour whenever the car broke down at home, since it had to be given first aid to get it over 120 miles of sand and mud to be repaired.

This could be dangerous work. Twice I cracked ribs, straining to reach the plugs, but Trevor Day killed himself while sealing a cracked petrol tank on his tractor; it exploded even though he had filled it with damp sand.

Building and demolition work that would have been done by contractors in England had to be done as best we could. When it was decided to transfer the Mission from the historic site to a new site, 20 miles away on the road to Choma, I had to demolish the old buildings with the help of a few local people. The pulpit from the old church was saved, and carried by boat across the floods. I sold the zincs from the roofs, neatly piled according to size, for £280. The beams that had supported them were made from mukwa, an iron-hard wood impervious to ants, and highly prized. I held two auctions, and raised enough cash to pay for a new church at the new site, because there was no money to spare from the Missionary Society for a church building after they had built new staff houses.

Getting the cash was one thing; actually building the church was quite another. Fortunately a new Anglican Cathedral had recently been built in

Bringing the new pulpit to New Kasenga

Lusaka. The fabric had been laid on to a metal skeleton. From a copy of the blueprint, I got a scaled-down version of the metal frame, 80 feet high, made by a local steel firm.

To dig out foundations and do the bricklaying, I hired a gang of refugees from the Congo. They made camp at the edge of the mission, and we set to work. When building schools, I had used clay, dug out and pressed into moulds, then baked hard in the sun. For the church, I bought breeze blocks from Lusaka. The workers were willing, but no more experienced than me. One day, I had to make a journey to Choma. I went carefully over the blueprint with the foreman, promising to be back the same evening. To demonstrate how well they could manage without me, they worked like slaves, and raised the wall up to roof level. Unfortunately, they forgot the window openings, and their work had to be demolished next day. The belfry tower was altogether beyond our powers, so I placed it on the ground near the front doors.

When the church was finished, the workmen celebrated with a big beer-drink. We listened happily to the sound of drumming and singing. Late in the evening, a worker hammered on our door. He had a knife sticking out of his shoulder. After Ena extracted it and dressed the wound, I went to the

The new church

camp with him to arrest his assailant. When we got there, my heart failed at the size of the crowd round the fire. I only had six bullets in the revolver in my pocket. However, they told me that the culprit had run off into the bush, and who was I to argue? I was glad to see the last of them when I paid them off two days later.

THE ROOT OF ALL EVIL

*M*oney caused all sorts of problems. There was a gap between our pay and that of our African colleagues for a start. Male missionaries were paid £15 per week, the same as ministers in England. Our wives, of course, received no pay for the 70-hour weeks that they worked. However, we did get perks, such as free medicines and dental and medical treatment from the English doctors, dentists and opticians.

African ministers were paid five pounds per week by the church, although they did the same work as us, and often were in charge of us. This situation was insoluble, and occasionally we felt guilty, but our colleagues never seemed to resent it.

Our chief means of raising money from our community, however, was

Collecting maize

the District Extension Fund, or DEF. A better name would have been "VHW", or Very Hard Work. In England, congregations support their churches by putting money on to the plates week by week. This is not possible in a subsistence farming community, so their contributions were in kind.

Every year after the rains I distributed sacks to each of the 60 villages in the area. In 1960, I had to buy 25 new ones at 25/ – each. This took many weeks. Each September I went round to collect the sacks, filled with maize. It was hard labour for a little chap like me. The grain was taken to be ground at Maala store, and sold to the Girl's School for £2 per bag. The total raised was £120, less the token charge made by Tony Jones for grinding.

HOW TO MAKE A
CHRISTIAN

The purpose of all our endeavours was to convert the Ila people to Christianity. We had a head start, because there was no such thing as an atheist among them. They all believed in Leza, the great God, high above all local spirits and lesser deities. They also loved telling and hearing stories, and listened willingly to all we told them about God's son, Jesus.

Naturally, this involved learning to speak their beautiful language. The Government awarded £20, a substantial sum, for passing the language exam. Previous missionaries had translated the New Testament and the Book of Psalms, and we also had the Catechism and the Offices in Ila. There were nevertheless snags to trap the unwary. I had to conduct Holy Communion regularly in the School. I noticed covert smiles on their faces when I recited the Gloria – "Holy, Holy, Holy, Lord God of hosts". Fortunately one girl took me aside and explained that I was saying "*Leza Usulula*" instead of "*Leza Usalala*". Look it up in my Dictionary.

I gave a regular monthly sermon to the two dozen prisoners in Namwala gaol. They had all been convicted of killing, since lesser offences were purged by fines or branding on the forehead. They were a model congregation, since I was the only form of entertainment provided for them.

Sometimes I preached at Baambwe village. This was the last of the old-style townships, with a stockade round a great ring of houses. The cattle were driven into the stockade every evening. I visited Baambwe soon after our arrival, to pay my respects to Chief Mukobela. I chose the wrong day to call, because everybody was lolling about in various stages of intoxication, after a big beer-drink. The chief was mortified, and promised that if I were to return a week later, I should find a sober audience. I spent great care on my sermon, writing it out in bold letters. When I arrived, Mukobela sent round his messengers to round everybody up, and the whole population was soon assembled, probably the largest congregation I had ever preached to.

The main work of preaching was carried out by our team of 44 Local Preachers, who conducted weekly services in 16 village centres. There were no church buildings, but we used schoolrooms or shady river banks.

In addition, the evangelism was carried out through the traditional Methodist system of Class Meetings. Kasenga Circuit covered an enormous area, and when the pioneer missionaries had explored it 60 years previously, they had selected about a dozen villages in which to establish weekly meetings on the traditional Methodist pattern. The Class Leaders went patiently through the Catechism, grafting Christian doctrine on to the native stock.

The women were ministered to by a sisterhood called *"Ruwadzano"*, "Red blouses". Their black skirts symbolised Sin, the red blouses the Blood of Jesus, and the white caps, "Salvation".

The whole system was run by a staff of three ministers: Mark Malyenkuku the Superintendent, me, and a young probationer minister called Wilmot Munyimba. We visited the classes as often as distance and floods permitted. We appointed a Colporteur, John Syangombe by name, who covered a wide area by cycle, selling Bibles. This was not a success. After a month or two, John decamped with all the takings. I received a letter from him sometime later, saying "We regret to inform you that mister John has passed away".

HOW MANY WIVES?

*P*olygamy remained the chief obstacle to our evangelism. Ila mothers breast fed their children up to the age of two or three years. During this period it was strictly taboo for them to have any sexual relations, hence the plurality of wives. Chief Mungaila married his 14th wife during our stay, and Chief Mukobela reputedly had dozens. Certainly, over 90 of his children were in our schools over the years.

Canon Law was framed for Europe and ill-fitted to Ila culture. One of our senior Local Preachers, Joshua Matale, took a second wife when his first became too old to look after him. In our terms, the new wife was a housekeeper, but there was no bending the rules, and I had to turn him away from the communion table. Many times, we missionaries tried to get the prohibition overturned, but our African colleagues turned it down as racial condescension. It was not until 1963 that the Synod grudgingly allowed certain exceptions.

It is thus not surprising that the largest section of our Christian community was composed of "Catechumens", or "members under instruction". However deep their faith in Jesus, and their allegiance to the church, they could never become Christians without repudiating their extra wives, which was virtually impossible in the Ila social setup. Just as the "Godfearers" in the Book of Acts accepted Jesus but stuck at circumcision, so these men could not in all decency throw their wives out to become outcasts from society.

Over the years I baptised 105 persons, nearly all teenagers or women. In addition, there were 154 existing members, 115 "On Trial", 582 Catechumen polygamists, and 248 young people in the various Sunday Schools. In other words, roughly 11% of the total population claimed to be Christian.

APPENDIX ONE:
WHY MISSIONARIES?

*W*hy did we become missionaries? Because it seemed to be the inevitable thing to do at the time. Oxford in 1949 was awash with religion. The Student Christian Movement (SCM) and the Oxford Inter-Collegiate Christian Union (OICCU) vied for undergraduate recruits, holding lunch-hour prayer meetings in town and colleges. Missions to the University used celebrities of the day. The University Church, St. Mary's, was packed every Sunday evening with undergraduates listening to famous evangelical preachers. Methodist undergraduates met on Sunday afternoons in "tea clubs" – Margaret Thatcher was a member of our club a year before we joined. Ena and I were both Methodist local preachers, and often took services in the villages round Oxford. So it was not strange that, when we graduated, we decided to spend our lives in Christian work. Ena, inspired by a stirring call from a missionary, went to the Methodist Missionary Society in London, where she was told to gain a practical qualification. She duly trained for a year at Homerton College in Cambridge to get a teaching certificate. My own "missionary call" was based on cold statistics, since it was clear that the need for qualified Christian workers was far greater in Central Africa than in England.

While Ena was training, I entered the Methodist Ministry, and started on a theology degree. We got married, and while I served my two years' probation in rural Derbyshire, Ena supported us both by teaching at a genteel school for young ladies.

After I was ordained, they sent us to Selly Oak Missionary College. Here I learned how to repair a car with chewing gum, porridge and stockings, while Ena learned how to cut hair and run a household in the tropics, also attending a course at the London School of Tropical Medicine. She gave birth to our firstborn daughter, after which we were finally launched on our missionary career.

APPENDIX TWO: THE ILA PEOPLE

*F*or thirty years the Ila papers remained untouched in the old suitcases, until on my retirement in 1994, I was able to begin work on them. To arrange, transcribe, and translate them occupied me for 6 years, until in the year 2000 I was able to publish a 900-page *"Dictionary of Ila Usage, 1860 – 1960"*.

We had lived with these Ila people as our closest neighbours for over six years, and I thought that we knew them well. But what appeared in my dictionary was not the bare list of words and meanings that I had expected. Here were the thoughts of individuals, their views on each other and on life in general, their humour and preoccupations in daily living. I began to sieve through the entries in the dictionary for key words and synonyms to use in a book about the Ila themselves. A surprising image emerged, or rather, a series of portraits like the snapshots in a family album. I arranged the sayings under themes, such as Manners, Raising a Family, The Spirit World. Two years later this emerged as a second book, called *The Ila Speaking, Records of a lost world*.

It disclosed a vanished civilisation. A selection of extracts from it follows, in which the translated Ila phrases are in italics.

MANNERS AND ETIQUETTE

*C*hildren were taught to respect their elders. *God does not like little children to stare at their elders.* Still less did God approve of rude noises and swearing. One old man said *Long ago, if someone swore at his seniors, they sold him to another chief.* When visiting friends, tact was needed. *We must eat this salad even if it is awful. The guest of Tortoise has to eat mushrooms.* After leaving their hosts, it was different: *On the way home from visiting, one is never short of something to be rude about.* The worst offence was to eat alone, without sharing: *So-and-so eats alone. He realises that when he eats with others he does not fill his belly, so he prefers to behave like a thief.* Such a man was called Sikasinalinso (*Mr. Eats-with-his eyes-shut*) or Sibonikumbi (the Sable antelope, *whose horns are so heavy that it never looks up*).

When eating, a bowl of maize porridge was placed on the ground, into which each person dipped his sop of meat to scoop out a mouthful. Promptness at meals was insisted on, and the proverb ran *Muteba smoked on, so his place went to another!* However, it was bad manners to display unseemly haste: *This one's jumping up and down like a cat waiting to be fed! Calm down, you'll have a heart attack!* Noisy or slovenly eaters were criticised: *This chap makes a squelching noise when he eats.* They had three separate words for traces of food left round the mouth. Is there one in English?

The absence of clothing and chairs made deportment very important: *When a woman sits down, she tucks her apron between her legs.* Little girls were told *Sit down properly. You've got your legs apart like a woman in labour.* A man ought not flop down with his bottom on the ground, nor cross his ankles like a tailor, but had to squat on his heels.

They had no latrines, so great care had to be taken when attending to the needs of nature. *Mr does-it-on-the-fence* was a timorous person who did not venture outside the village at night. A woman who refused to take good advice would be called *She who goes about with "it" on the back of her skirt.*

Everyday conversation was governed by a strict set of rules. It was forbidden to speak one's own name, or the name of one's father or mother or sister-in-law. A husband could not use his wife's name, nor she her husband's; they could not even use words that sounded like their names. A man had even to refer to his own son as *My father's namesake.* "Kusontomoka" means both to *use a name wrongly* and *to fall flat on one's face.*

As for rude words, well! *If a man mentions faeces in front of women, they will fine him, saying "Pay up, you used a dirty word! Why ever did you mention faeces in our presence?"* The careful man even avoided saying the names of the Knob-billed Goose or the Pallah, because they resembled the names of certain bodily parts: *If you use that word, you'll be told "As penalty for your indecency, you must not eat today. Your wife will not let you eat. Even if it comes to blows, it's you they'll curse!"*

Insults were of two kinds: facetious ones used in friendly banter, and deadly ones intended to provoke. Examples of the former kind: *You fool! You really died at birth, because they buried the baby by mistake, and kept the after-birth! Your head's as big as a cow's! You haven't enough urine in you to put a match out! Your belly sticks out as though you'd swallowed boulders or were having twins.*

Nobody took such badinage seriously. But the other kind was meant to lead to blows: *He reviled his neighbour and abused him. He called him a foul name, saying "You are a bastard, son of a slave-girl bought for a bag of salt!"* One day in Kafue Training Institute, a junior boy shouted an insulting epithet at a senior, who happened to be a Mwila. It took three of us to rescue the abuser, who was almost throttled to death. The Ila boy explained rather huffily that he had been mortally insulted by a forbidden word.

LOVE AND COURTSHIP

*W*hat made a man say of a girl "*Mucono*" (She's lovely)? The glow of health on a young face was attractive, and so was nice hair: *The girls have a great new hairstyle. Their plaits reach down to their shoulders and they look lovely.* Short girls were not admired: *She's much too short. He shakes his head. She won't do, she doesn't suit him.*

Ila men did not favour the skinny western model. "*She's as skinny as a bulb! She's scrawny as a baling ladle!* Another was so thin, *she's as skinny round the waist as a wasp!* It was a compliment to say to a girl: *You're plump as a pumpkin, your hips are as broad as a meat-tray!*

On the other hand, plump men were not admired. *He's a fine man. You'll find he has a flat stomach and perfect manners. He's really good-looking and altogether terrific!* Less fortunate men had to work harder: *He draws in his stomach like someone fording a flood.*

Strangely enough, there are more references to men's faces than to women's. *He has an ugly face: it's flat.* Of another: *This man is ugly; his face looks screwed up.* We should expect a one-eyed man, or one with pock marks, to be thought ugly, but it's strange to learn that too dark a complexion was not liked: *This man's face is as black as a sable antelope's!* Of one poor man it was recorded *His face is so repulsive that nobody ever looks at it twice!*

Some men seemed to attract women without effort. *He's lucky. Women chase after him! He has no need for blankets.* Perhaps it was because *His body is shiny: he's a real dandy.* Some spent hours grooming themselves and were gently mocked: *The dandy has moved his bangle round so much that he's run out of arms and legs to put it on!* Another who was late for meals was told: *We've eaten all the food now, you took so long polishing yourself!*

Celibacy was not unknown, but the fact that the same word meant "celibacy" and "slavery" is revealing. An unmarried man was called

"*Situpumpu*" (No fingers) or *Sikolo* (manual labourer). *A bachelor's like a labourer; he has to look after himself because he has no wife.* It was the same with women: *This woman is a half-wit; she does not want to get married!*

In some cases, a man's parents would arrange a bride, but often a man would do his own wooing. Any young man travelling about might be asked *Are you looking for a pot?* Parents of marriageable girls would be on guard against frivolous callers, and a suitor would be strictly interviewed. He would be careful to remain standing, even if offered a stool. *You who want to marry, have you a fish-spear more than a year old?* He answers *I have. Have you an axe to work with? I have.* When they were satisfied that he was properly respectful and doing things correctly, they would give him their daughter.

If the girl was still a child, he would leave a deposit of a cow, and give her a new outfit. The girl would have marital status even before she had gone through initiation and been collected by her suitor.

ILA RHYMES & SONGS
(TRANSLATED AND VERSIFIED BY ENA)

A mother would dangle her baby on her knees and hold each of his fingers in turn, while she sang *"Kantengeza, kantengeza"*:

Little finger, little finger, who's your younger brother?
This little finger is mummy of them all,
This finger sleeps in the middle like a mouse.
This finger's mummy, who feeds all the house,
This one's the thumb, the thumby-thumb-thumb.
Pumpkin's come! Pumpkin's come! (making his fists into a ball).

In 1985 we went to visit 85-year-old Andrew Dale, who had come to England for an operation. I gave him a copy of the book, and his eye fell on the rhyme. "Ah, 'Kantengeza, Kantengeza,'", he laughed. "My mother used to sing that to me on her knee."

To lull her baby to sleep, she would sing this lullaby:

Wezu mwana, ulalilanzi? *This little baby, why does he cry?*
Ulalila impande yakwabo. *He cries for the moon shell up in the sky!*
Nomwangule! *Get it down from way up high!*
Twalela! *We'll feed him with it by and by.*

A toddler would hold up both fists clenched, and as each name was chanted, the finger was unbent. On ten, the hands were clapped together:

> *I am counting,*
> *Let me count two,*
> *This little corncob's bigger than you!*
> *Baby's squashed up, next to me,*
> *He's biting my knuckle!*
> *Let me be!*
> *And here's the Wildcat;*
> *Cat's not bunched up,*
> *Old man's hunched up,*
> *This is number ten!*

Older children who had been initiated by having their front teeth knocked out would chant:

> *You with the teeth,*
> *You with the teeth,*
> *Poo, poo, poo!*
> *Whoever died from teeth knocked out?*
> *You'll turn into a zebra-snout!*

Children love to mimic, and this was one game they loved. They would walk round in procession, hobbling and stooping like old Polyoko, chanting:

> *Polyoko, Polyoko, through the woods we went a walk-o.*
> *Polyoko, Polyoko, Alas, alack, I cracked my back,*
> *Bending low down for my walk-o!*

Older girls would mimic diviners contacting spirits, and shut themselves in a house to chant:

> *Ulu, the spectres are come!*
> *Ulu, the ghosties come!*
> *Don't shut me in, don't shut me in,*
> *They'll shave my head before they're done!*

Travelling songs

These were sung to encourage weary porters. One would improvise, and the rest respond:

> *They rise up far away, those landmarks.*
> *They are far off, far away!*
> *Yet I shall pass them!*
> *They are like a barrier ahead.*
> *Yet later there will be a pass!*
> The next one is wrily humorous:
> *If I don't pass those hills yonder*
> *I'll go on for ever!*
> *But if my leg explodes into bits*
> *I'll never get there!*

Fishing songs

Fishing was not a hobby, but a vital activity:

> *My fish-spear has saved my children from starvation.*

Fishing rights were jealously guarded from neighbouring tribes like the Bambala:

> *You Bambala, here are fishing waters.*
> *Here are the pools where one must fish.*
> *But, Bambala, you are foreigners.*
> *We shall kill you wherever you fish!*

When William Chapman was first exploring the Kasenga area to find a site for the projected mission, he witnessed an example of this. "We passed a small pool one day, where two men were fishing. Presently several others came and claimed the sole right to fish in it, and without any compunction whatever they at once speared the two poor fellows to death.

By the time we went to live at Kasenga, the Kafue fishing had passed into the hands of people from Nyasaland, who had a summer colony at Kasenga, and the arrangement was accepted.

Drinking songs

Men tramping along to a beer-drink would chorus:

> Twafwa itiki, twafwa itiki, *We're dying for a ticky, dying for a ticky!*
> Ikubi leli likasike lili? *When is the party starting, Micky?*
> Twafwa itiki, twafwa itiki! *We're dying for a ticky, dying for a ticky!*
> Tukasobane! *Let's have fun at the beer-drink, Micky!*

The ticky was the smallest silver coin, good for two Ila organic eggs or a flagon of beer. Beer-drinks could be quite small, as when an enterprising wife decided to raise some cash by brewing. Others, for funerals, could be big affairs drawing guests from a wide area. There was always a funeral going on somewhere, and some men seemed to spend most of their time searching out beer-drinks:

> *We're knackered, going on without rest.*
> *We're going from pillar to post, it's killing us finding beer-drinks!*

Funeral songs

> *Hey there, kiddo, scrape up the ash, you.*
> *Happy, I'm happy, I can tell you!*
> *My father's namesake calls its calf up.*
> *Me, I flop down, then I try to bounce up!*

The "Father's namesake" was the dead man's guardian spirit, and the "calf" was the dead man. The "ash" of the roasting fires was scraped up at the end of a week's feasting. This hints at how the Ila coped with death. They mourned and hoped. The merry celebration was at once a mark of respect to the dead, and a defiance of the terrors of the unknown. The singer had a sense of the spiritual world which may or may not be the answer to the awful event they are celebrating, yet the other lines show a state of legless insobriety.

Here is a touching dirge sung by a poor man stricken by the death of his mother, carrying her body to the grave:

Ndukuya buzimya, *Carry her I must,*
Ubuli bakando bezi maanu. *Like the wise old men.*
Ndaya buzimya, Mama wezu. *Carry her I will, to the dust, my mother.*

FUNERALS

*E*veryone dressed up for a big funeral. Men carried elaborate wands called "*Sizanza*". One man makes his from a bunch of feathers, one from palm leaves, another from the tail of an eland. A woman would wear an elaborate belt of fine skin with bells attached. Each mourner would present a gift – a fat-pan, a churn, spears, even an ox.

Next the grave was dug. This was no easy thing, as it had to be big enough to take the body, seated in a chair. The site was sometimes a matter of dispute. One notorious incident occurred at Nsante when the chief died. The villagers quarrelled so about the site that in the end they cut the body in two and had two burials at different places. (Ever afterwards, they were called "*Banamwaabane*", (Dividers).

When the grave was filled in, the widows threw themselves on it, wailing and ullulating. The men held a mock combat, marching back and forth with spears raised. At such a funeral, two hundred cattle might be killed. Driven into the village clearing, they would stand quietly while the spearmen darted up and threw spears. They would be stuck like a pincushion before slowly subsiding without protest. They were butchered on the spot, and the dripping portions handed out to all comers.

The funeral feast might last for days, or even weeks. Prodigious quantities of beef and beer were consumed on the spot, and further beer drinks for the dead man were held at intervals. A few weeks after the ashes had been swept up came the beer of the spears, next the beer of the homecoming, next the beer of the offerings. Finally came the beer of the weeping, on the anniversary, and the funeral was finally over.

Such voices from another age reveal not only the preoccupations of daily existence in Ila villages over a century ago, but an outlook both sensitive and wrily humorous. Feared in battle, fearful of spirits, revering God; hunters of lion and buffalo, polygamous, romantic; ribald in men's company, but highly proper in women's; tender towards children; highly esteeming the arts of hospitality. ***TULI BAILA!***

Appendix Three: Ila tenses (a new approach by Ena Fowler, M.A. Oxon.)

1. Edwin Smith's *Handbook*

hough President of the Royal Anthropological Society and foremost authority on the Ila nation and its culture, he confessed himself baffled by the contrast between their primitive savagery and their sophisticated language. He writes of "the extraordinary richness and flexibility of the language. It is a fine instrument; it has potentialities far beyond their need of self-expression..." (Smith and Dale, vol.2, p.310)

In 1907 he published the first full grammar of Ila, *A Handbook of the Ila Language*. Amazing as was the extent of his knowledge and scholarship, the one flaw was that he was misled by the fashion of the time for using the pattern of Latin and Greek as the skeleton structure for Ila.

First, the teaching method was inappropriate. Each tense in Latin has its own characteristic infix. Within each tense there are six possible variations according to person, supplied by suffixes. Therefore to list the tenses one by one, each with a six-person conjugation, was a very suitable method for teaching Latin.

In Ila, however, the same few infixes and just one suffix, added or subtracted as required, are used for all the tenses and moods. Within each tense it is not the person of the verb but the class of the noun that affects the conjugation. The manipulation of three vowels (*a,e,u*) and two consonants (*l* and *k*) is all that is needed to provide most of the meanings conveyed by the Latin indicative, subjunctive and passive moods in any tense. What is needed is not a Latin framework, but to learn the noun classes and understand the manipulation of *a,e,u* and *k*.

Secondly, his tense names, based on Latin and Greek tense names, did not correspond with the Ila constructions, for reasons which will be seen later. He was very sensitive to the nuances of the verbs, but found that he had opened a Pandora's box when it came to finding names for them.

He identified in the *Handbook* twenty-four tenses in the indicative mood active, namely three present tenses, three imperfects, three aorists, four pasts, two perfects, one pluperfect, two immediate futures and six futures. In addition he listed five tenses in the potential mood and four in the subjunctive, not to mention twenty negatives and four imperatives (Smith 1907: 146 – 175).

By the time he wrote his notes for a revision of the *Handbook* he had found even more tenses. Revising page 146 he spoke of a 'hypothetical' tense and a 'rather' tense. Revising page 157 he mentioned a 'future pluperfect', giving as examples *balakusulene* and *ulakubatwele*. Revising page 161 he wrote 'Another tense? - a present progressive continuative *mulakufwa* "you will go on dying" '.

Some of the proliferation was due to Smith's criteria for naming a new tense. Different constructions using the same tense were considered to be different tenses. Tenses 3, 5, 6, 8, 9, 12, 13, 16, 18, 23 and 24 of table 1 were already-listed tenses using an additional *ci* or *bu*. They should not have been named as separate tenses. His 'rather' tense was the imperative with an adverb added.

One can see Smith's puzzlement growing as each tense name had to be qualified by footnotes. 'Generally the immediate future, *Ndi la bona*, or the aorist *Nda bona*, is used with a present meaning' (Smith 1907:147). Of the 'past imperfect' tense he wrote: 'This tense denotes what was being done at some past time. It may also take place shortly' (Smith 1907:149). Of the 'aorist': 'We call this tense the aorist, but in Ila it does not always denote what is absolutely past. In fact, with slight changes in accent, it may express anything, past, present, or future' (Smith 1907:151). It is obvious from his revision notes that he himself was rather dubious about some of the names he had given. Revising page 161, section 2, he said of what he called the future subjunctive no. 2 (3rd p. *akubona*): 'Is not this more a tense indicating continuation?'. In revising page 162, with reference to 'future subjunctive no. 4' (3rd p. *akakubona*) he said: 'Is not this more a continuative tense?'.

Smith and his colleague John Price had unrivalled knowledge of the language. They left at Kasenga Mission over 12,000 vocabulary cards, each bearing a different word with examples of its use, patiently gathered over the years from the local people. Yet, mesmerised by the classics, Smith did not realise that language 'rules' are no more than observed patterns, and should be the servants, not the masters, of a language system. He did not see that the patterns of a language dominated by person-driven conjugations and case-driven declensions were not at all suitable for another language that was motivated by the poetry of alliteration, assonance, rhythm and tone, and by ideas that could move around the verb at will.

TABLE 1: SMITH'S 24 TENSES REDUCED IN NUMBER

Subj. Conc. 3rd p.s. e.g					Present stem	or Perfect stem
u					bona	
u	l	a	ka		bona	
u	l	a			bona	
u–		a			bona	
(u–		a)	ka		bona	
(u–		a)	ka			bwene
U	l	a(a)		ku	bona	
u–		a(a)		ku	bona	
u–		a(a)		ku		bwene

Tense	No.
Present' (used in relative clauses)	1
Immediate Future' (*also* present) 'Future Tense 1'	17 19
Aorist' (any of Past/ Present/Future) 'Future Tense 3'	7 21
'Past or Preterite' 'Future Tense 2'	10 20
'Past Tense: Another Form' (*also* Preterite/Pluperfect Present)	11
'Future Tense 4'	22
'Past Imperfect'	4
'Pluperfect' (*also* Imperfect)	15

Notes

i) When 1 does not intervene between the subjectival concord and the particle *a, u-a > wa.*

ii) Tense 19: 'Future Tense 1': Smith wrote it as *ukalabona.*

iii) Tense 11: 'Past Tense: Another Form': this form was translated as a preterite ('He did see') by Smith. The subjectival concord may be omitted altogether in the noun class 1s (Smith) or class 1 (Hopgood).

iv) Tense 22: 'Future Tense 4' Smith wrote it as *ulaya ku bona,* but the prevalent form in Fowler 2000 is *ulaaku* (*bona,* etc.).

v) 'Subj. Conc.' = 'Subjectival Concord'.

2.A NEW APPROACH TO IDENTIFYING THE TENSES

Some of the twenty-four tenses in the indicative active listed by Smith in the *Handbook* may be removed: the tenses containing *ci* or *bu* may be omitted for the reasons explained above. The tenses of the verb 'to be' (*kuli*) are also left out.

The number of tenses is now nine instead of twenty-four. Listed with identical infixes underneath one another, showing only one of their many subjectival concords, they begin to reveal an interesting pattern (table 1).

The tense names in quotation marks in table 1 are those given by Smith. The other names I added after finding examples of their use in Fowler 2000. In the right-hand column is the number by which Smith identified the tense in the *Handbook*. As a sample subjectival concord, *u* has been chosen. This is the 3rd person singular of the most common noun class, that used for a person. It is class 1s in Smith's noun system, class 1 in Hopgood's noun system. The form is not seen clearly in written Ila unless the letter **l** intervenes. The spelling disguises the form, e.g. *u-a* is written as *wa, li-a* as *lya, i-a* as *ya, si-a* as *sya, bu-a* as *bwa, ku-a* as *kwa, lu-a* as *lwa, tu-a* as *twa.* Alternatively, assimilation takes place, e.g. *ci-a>ca.*

The heading 'present or perfect stem' is not totally accurate. The 'present' stem is used with the present, future, aorist and past tenses.

By writing only once the particles used, table 1 can be expressed even more simply:

Table 2: A reduced form of Table 1

Subjectival Concord 3rd p. sing	Add one or more of:	Root	Ending
U etc.	la a ka/ku	e.g. bon	*a* or perfect suffix

i)When **l** does not intervene between u and a, u-a>wa.

ii) Some perfect suffixes are formed simply by changing the final *a* to *e*, *ele* or *ile*. With other verbs modifications occur also in the root (e.g. inf. *kukala*, p.p. *kele*, *kubona*, p.p. *bwene*).

To clarify even further, we can look at the 'aorist tense' alone (table 3).

Table 3: The aorist

Subjectival Concord 3rd p. sing.	The aorist	Root	Final *a*
e.g. *u*	*a*	*bon*	*a*

There is a very simple yet utterly flexible structure that would account for the tenses observed by Edwin Smith, as follows.

The letter *a* that designates the 'aorist tense' is a 'jack-of-all-trades'. It simply announces a happening, in past, present or future. Unless further guidance is given, the listener may understand by *a* whatever tense is suitable. This is demonstrated by the following sentences and translations:

Wa(=u-a)-bona! You see!
Wa(=u-a)-ceensya　　　　He is exaggerating.
Wa(=u-a)-ceensya　　　　He exaggerated.
Wa(=u-a)-bona mapopwe? Have you seen the
　　　　　　　　　　　　maize?
Nda(=ndi-a)-fwa compankowe　I was dying of
　　　　　　　　　　　　　　shyness.[1]

If further clarification is required, the manipulation of two consonants (**l** and *k*), and two vowels (*e* and *u*) gives further details – in fact, almost the whole body of information provided by the tenses, moods and voices of Latin. *A* is used as a 'separator' between the meaningful consonants.

The letter **l** may be called a 'definer'. It defines the present or immediate future (see table 1). It is the only letter that signifies a time rather than an idea.

The letter *k* has a different function. It is what might be called a 'mover'. When there is no **l** to indicate the future, *k* moves the tense either forwards or backwards in time, according to pronunciation, says Smith (Smith 1907: 157). A second *k* moves the tense even further forwards or backwards in time. *K* may even suggest that the event may not take place at all. Smith called this construction the potential mood.

In addition to **l** and *k*, the vowel *u* is significant. If the separating vowel after *k* is *u* instead of *a*, *ku* simply suggests continuity, in any tense, so it is not a tense-forming particle. *Ku* is used also for other purposes: as a preposition, or to reduce an over-long sentence, to emphasise, to express purpose.

After the root come particles known as 'derivatives' or verbal species', one or more of which may be used to give additional meanings. These derivatives include the letter *w*, which perhaps should have been written as *u*; this transforms the verb from active to passive.

The verb is usually brought to an end in one of three ways:
1 by the letter *a;*
2 a letter *e* following certain kinds of imperative, or a clause of purpose or possibility (rather like the Latin subjunctive);

3 by a perfect stem. This is formed by a change to the suffix. The vowel preceding the suffix may also change, normally according to the following pattern: *a-a>e-e, e-a>e-e, i-a>i-e, o-a>o-ele, u-a>u-ile or uwile*. The perfect stem fulfils one of two functions:

  i) it signifies a state 'resultant upon a completed action' (Doke 1935: 163), or

  ii) it moves the time further into the past, e.g.

wakaakufumba	he was scratching,
*wakaakufumb**ile***	he had scratched.

3. A NEW APPROACH TO UNDERSTANDING THE TENSES

It is not surprising that in table 1 the list of tenses with meanings is chaotic. The meanings of Latin verbs were as though written on tablets of stone. Certain spellings always referred to past time, others always to the present, others to the future; also there were stylised patterns and combinations found, for example, in conditional sentences.

Ila verbs are different. They are more like clouds or birds. The same few particles fly hither and thither, serve different purposes, appear and disappear, and change the significance of a verb to its opposite. Only one letter, *l*, defines a set time - almost. It actually defines two times, not one, namely either present or immediate future.

Of the other important letters, *k* and *u* convey *ideas*: times relative to other times ('later than', 'earlier than') or the length of time (continuously or not). *E* is used either to express ideas or to move times, as described above. The verbal species, mostly two-letter particles, provide an absolute feast of ideas: causation, reciprocity, potentiality, intensity, reversal, repetition and passivity.

This is why Latin tense names and Ila spellings cannot be equated. It is easy, however, to understand Ila if not **tense names**, but **ideas only**, are held in the mind. Different combinations of ideas are chosen at will from the following selection:

Something is happening/has happened – but when? And how?

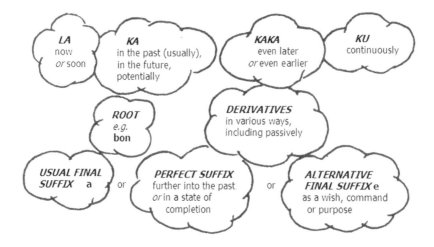

The result is a very succinct language. For example, Smith translates the six-syllabled verb *balakusulene* by a sentence of fourteen words, 'They not only hate one another now but will continue to do so always'. The verb may be broken down as follows:

ba	subjectival concord
la	(something is happening) in the present or near future
ku	(something is happening or will happen) continuously
sulene	the perfect stem (root + suffix) of the verb
kusulana ('to hate one another'), incorporating the	
	verbal derivative *an*.

If the particles forming a verb are seen as stand-alone ideas, then endless combinations may be understood by the listener without strain.

With the verbs cut down in number from Smith's original list as previously explained, ignoring the negatives and the separate pattern of the workings of the verb 'to be', it is now possible to devise a table (table 4 on page 139) which embraces not only the variety of tenses in the indicative mood, but also all the subjectival concords (also called subject personal pronouns) for 1st, 2nd and 3rd persons, the derivatives (also called verbal species) including the passive, and the potential and subjunctive moods.

Table 4 is spectacularly simple, given the number of variations theoretically possible for any one verb, over 5000 (14 subjectival concords x 6 verbal infixes x 20 derivatives x 3 endings). Once we have stopped thinking 'Such-and-such a spelling forms such-and-such a tense', and start thinking 'That particle conveys such-and-such an idea', a language that has been seen as very complicated can be understood with ease. In this, as in other respects, it is a remarkable language

Table 4: The structure of Ila verbs

Use one of:	Add 1 or more of:	Add	Add if required:	Add 1 of:
Subjectival concord (s.p.p.)			Root Derivative infixes: (v e r b a l species)	
ndi	la a ka/ku	Root		a
a				
ba			el	e
ka			en	
i			il	Perfect
ci			in	suffix
li			y	
si			sy	
u			zy	
bu			an	
ku			ok	
lu			uk	
mu			ek	
tu			ik	
			esy	
			isy	
			on	
			ul	
			un	
			elel	
			ulul	
			(i)w	

Notes on Table 4

i) The subjectival concords change as follows when there is no intervening **l** :
  bu-a>bwa, ci-a>ca, i-a>ya, ku-a>kwa, li-a>lya, lu-a>lwa, ndi-a>nda, tu-a>twa, u-a> wa, si-a>sya.

ii) The list of subjectival concords (also referred to as s.p.p. or subject personal pronouns) includes the 1st, 2nd and 3rd person. In the subjunctive mood, the s.p.p. of the 3rd p.s. of Smith's Class 1s noun (e.g. *muntu*) changes from **u** to **a**.

iii) This is the basic order of particles, but there are variations, e.g. in the future tense the two syllables of *laka* may be transposed to form *kala*. In Smith's tenses nos. 10 and 11 the subjectival concord may appear after *ka* instead of before *ka*; in the 3rd p.s. it may even be omitted altogether in noun class 1s (Smith) or class l (Hopgood).

These examples were supplied by Mr. P. K. Likukela.

ACKNOWLEDGEMENTS

My thanks are due, as ever, to Paul Smith, without whose help and encouragement this memoir would never have seen the light of day.

Lightning Source UK Ltd.
Milton Keynes UK
UKOW07f1911181115

263018UK00010B/49/P